Golf Shops, Coffee Shops & Barber Shops

Chris Rowe

Paperback ISBN: 978-1-64719-234-1
Hardcover ISBN: 978-1-64719-235-8
Epub ISBN: 978-1-64719-236-5
Mobi ISBN: 978-1-64719-237-2

Published by BookLocker.com, Inc., St. Petersburg, Florida.

Printed on acid-free paper.

BookLocker.com, Inc.
2021

DISCLAIMER

This book details the author's personal experiences with and opinions about golf.

The author and publisher are providing this book and its contents on an as is" basis and make no representations or warranties of any kind with respect to this book or its contents. The author and publisher disclaim all such representations and warranties, including for example warranties of merchantability and professional advice for a particular purpose. In addition, the author and publisher do not represent or warrant that the information accessible via this book is accurate, complete or current.

The statements made about products and services have not been evaluated by the U.S. government. Please consult with your own legal, accounting, medical, or other licensed professional regarding the suggestions and recommendations made in this book.

Except as specifically stated in this book, neither the author or publisher, nor any authors, contributors, or other representatives will be liable for damages arising out of or in connection with the use of this book. This is a comprehensive limitation of liability that applies to all damages of any kind, including (without limitation) compensatory; direct, indirect or consequential damages; loss of data, income or profit; loss of or damage to property and claims of third parties.

You understand that this book is not intended as a substitute for consultation with a licensed medical, legal or accounting professional. Before you begin any change your lifestyle in any way, you will consult a licensed professional to ensure that you are doing what's best for your situation.

This book provides content related to golf topics. As such, use of this book implies your acceptance of this disclaimer.

DEDICATION

To my boys: Regardless of how many books or how many awards you win along this journey my greatest accomplishment and reward is being your dad.

To Mom and Dad: Thank you for bringing me up in a Christian environment and giving me the tools to succeed in life. None of the great things in my life would have been possible without your love and support.

To Cambi: Thank you for always being proud of me and giving unconditional encouragement in life and my career. My life is better with you by my side and your smile is contagious for everyone who is lucky enough to meet you.

To God: For instilling a desire and love for the game of golf and the blessings received along the way. Absolutely not deserving or earned but blessed more than I deserve.

TABLE OF CONTENTS

FORWARD

How did the book title Golf Shops, Coffee Shops and Barbershops come about? When thinking about the title for my third book it became clear these places are where conversations take place every day. Spending almost thirty years now in the golf industry I've heard some great stories and have found, much like barbershops and coffee shops people tend to gather not only for the service these establishments provide, but for the conversations and comradery as well. Working at Colonial Country Club for ten years we would consistently have members come drink coffee and tell stories before they drove to work. I've noticed the same thing happens in barbershops when getting my haircut or walking into the local Starbucks and see the same thing. The stories told and the laughs had in the golf shop make coming to work fun because you see so many different customers come through the door every day. Putting these stories and ideas on paper allows me to be creative and get my ideas, along with some life experiences told. Golf is much like life because you never know what the next day may bring. One thing is for sure, bunkers are much like life, leave them both better than you found it while telling a few stories along the way. Hope you enjoy Golf Shops, Coffee Shops and Barbershops.

ALL BACKSWINGS ARE NOT CREATED THE SAME

Last weekend these four guys teed it up at Seminole Golf Club for a charity match. Between the four of them they've currently won five majors and numerous PGA & NCAA tournaments. Most players want to have their swing look perfect and hit all the positions, but what is really considered perfect? The perfect golf swing is the one you can consistently repeat with good results! Dustin Johnson, bends his left wrist at the top of his backswing with a shut clubface. Ricky Fowler, has a laid off backswing with a flat left wrist. Matt Wolff, crosses the line at the top of his swing with a slightly cupped left wrist. Rory, well he is perfect at the top of his backswing in terms of having the club on his shoulder plane with a square clubface position.

How can all four of these guys be world-class players and have such different backswings? The answer is they all end up in the same place at impact! It doesn't matter how you get to the top as long as you can get to impact the same as these guys!

ANGER

This past summer our family vacation was spent in Jamaica. If you haven't been to Jamaica, it's a wonderful place to visit with pristine beaches and beautiful water. One of the things that are most important to me is building memories with my kids. You can buy your kids all the stuff in the world, but stuff doesn't create memories. When we arrived in Jamaica we were exhausted from the travel and couldn't wait to get something to eat. The resort was massive with so many different restaurant options. We all knew one of the nights we would definitely be eating Japanese cooked table side.

The next day I went to our concierge to make reservations for each night during our stay. The Japanese restaurant was available the next night, so we booked it and spent the day snorkeling. We made our way to the restaurant that evening and sat at a cooking table with numerous people we had never met. Everyone sitting at the table was in a great mood with the chef telling jokes and preparing the food. A few minutes before the chef started to cook a couple arrived late and sat down at the last two seats around our table. The chef had given all of us nicknames and the mood was light, except for the new couple. This couple looked like they were in their mid-sixties and didn't seem like they were having a good night. You could tell very quickly the woman was excited to be eating and conversing with everyone around the cooking table, but the husband wanted nothing to do with any of us. All of a sudden, the husband through a complete temper tantrum on his wife and completely embarrassed her. He told the chef he was leaving and took his wife's hand and walked out of the restaurant. We were all stunned, and the mood was drastically changed for a few minutes. I reassured the chef he had done nothing wrong and the guy was obviously an unhappy person.

The interesting thing about this anger outburst was seeing this guy at the resort everywhere we went the rest of the week. The majority of the restaurant witnessed this and I'm not sure if he noticed, but every time we saw him my boys pointed out that's the guy who acted awful at dinner

On the golf course we all know that guy who complains or throws clubs. Don't be that person who everyone avoids because of a bad temper. Golf is already hard enough without beating yourself up over a shot. Remember even if you are sorry and apologize for an outburst on the golf course, everyone at the club is talking about you.

We had an absolute great vacation, but my boys still remember this guy acting the way he did at the cooking table as much as they remember snorkeling in the pristine waters of Jamaica. The next time you have the urge to throw your club or have a cussing outburst think about the guy in Jamaica and don't be that guy!

ATHLETES WHO FUDGE THEIR HEIGHT

How many times have you seen a football or basketball player listed at a height taller than they really are? Everyone knows how big of an Oklahoma Sooner fan I am, but Kyler Murray is shorter than listed in the program. Why do these athletes do this? The answer is simple they want to have their height taller because 6'0 sounds better than 5'11. Your handicap sounds better as a single digit than it does at double digit and your golf pro calls this a vanity handicap. We all know what a sandbagger is and none of us enjoy playing golf with these guys, but a vanity handicap is a misrepresentation as well.

This year turn in every score and try you're hardest to shoot the best round you can. If you have a horrible day on the course turn the score in regardless of the embarrassment. You are hurting yourself by misrepresenting your handicap and nobody will want you on their team, but I promise they will all want an individual bet.

BACCARAT

We have all seen James Bond play Baccarat in the movies and if you have been to Las Vegas you have seen the tables throughout the casinos. When you walk by a Baccarat table and see gamblers bending the cards or using the scorecard to track each session you would think this must be a difficult game. The reality is it is the same as betting heads or tails in a coin toss. You do not have to pick another card or stay like in the game Blackjack. The dealer does everything and all you do is pick which side you think will win. The Baccarat scorecards are used to track patterns that occur in the game. These scorecards are marked with the letter P for player and B for bank and T for tie. So, what does Baccarat have to do with your golf game? Two things you can take from this casino favorite to help your golf scores.

Just like in Baccarat you have patterns that develop the same as you have on your golf scorecard. Keeping track of how many Players or Banks on your Baccarat scorecard can be used in the same way with your golf scorecard to track fairways and greens hit. When you finish your round of golf and you have tracked your stats you will see a pattern develop. If you note L for a tee shot missed left and R for tee shot missed right and C for hit fairway you can track your driving stats. Marking the scorecard with H for hit green also allows you to understand the pattern of how many greens in regulation you hit in the round. There is usually a correlation with hitting fairways that correlates to hitting more greens. When you keep your stats, it is advantageous to show them to your instructor to help formulate a plan to improve.

The second lesson you can take from Baccarat and use to your advantage in golf is the idea that five times in a row the bank has won so the next time the player must win. News flash the cards have no idea what side you are betting! If you make two birdies in a row on the golf course, why can't you make another one for three in a row? The golf ball does not know how many birdies you have made. When you use superstition as logic on the golf course or in the casino you probably are losing at both.

Keep your stats for greens and fairways hit and never get superstitious on the course because your golf ball does not know the difference and neither do the cards in Baccarat. Vegas did not build all those hotels on winners so practice your golf game and find a few pigeons to play for a few bucks on the links!

CHANGING LANES

Most of us have vehicles with safety features built in. We have the screen that comes on when backing up. The feature that pulls the car back into your lane if you cross over. The tire pressure monitors that alerts when a tire reaches an inflation standard below normal. These features keep us safe and have probably saved thousands of accidents from happening.

The feature that always makes me have a bit of distrust is the light that flashes when a car is close to you in another lane. This feature covers the blind side, so you do not change lanes when a car is next to you. The challenge with this feature is you cannot see the car but trust the safety feature is giving you the correct information. One thing I have told my kids is to always look before changing lanes regardless if the safety light is blinking or not. Taking a double look so to speak is always better than chancing moving into another lane and hitting another vehicle. Our first look should be sufficient to trust, but to take that chance without looking in the mirror along with physically looking to see if another vehicle is in the other lane could mean disaster.

When you get to the green after your approach shot most people only look at the line of the putt from behind the ball. Sometimes you get the proper read and sometimes you completely miss read the putt. How many times have you badly misread a putt and notice the reason when you go to the other side of the hole to hit your next putt? When you go to the opposite side of the hole and look from a different direction you sometimes you confirm what you saw standing behind the ball and sometimes you see something different. Taking a second look is always a good thing because it gives your eyes the ability to see both sides of the putt line. Just like double checking to make sure another vehicle is not in your turn lane even though your safety feature does not detect another vehicle does not mean you should not physically look. I have missed a lot of putts after looking from the opposite side of the hole and seeing the contour of the slope so why take the chance and not confirm from both sides. My driving history is better than my putting history because I always look both ways when driving.

You will probably make more putts if you look both ways and you will be a safer driver if you do the same!

CHANGING YOUR BRAKES

Sometimes we think something is wrong with our swing and book a three-hour lesson with our golf pro asking for a major overhaul. If your brakes are squeaking that doesn't necessarily mean you need new brakes. You might have brake dust built up or may need an adjustment on your pads, but you might not need an entire brake job. Go through a checklist before you roll into the dealership and ask them for something you might not need. Your golf swing you might be off, and it could be as simple as standing too close to the ball or your alignment being off. You obviously don't need to change your entire swing if a minor adjustment could fix the problem. We all have to change our brakes at some point, but don't overhaul everything if you only need a minor adjustment.

CHASING THE NEXT SWING CURE

How many times have you found yourself watching golf on a Sunday afternoon and listened to the broadcaster talk about the new technique the player is working on with his coach?

Is there really a new and improved method that is radically going to change your game? There is no cookie cutter solution to a golf swing, but everyone on the PGA Tour chases the next hot idea. My main man, Bryson DeChambeau now looks like the hulk and is slashing away at the ball with massive distance gains. I'm not sure everyone on tour will go to the extremes that Bryson goes, but many will if he has success. Do you remember stack & tilt, natural golf, X factor and all the other teaching techniques that have come along in the past few decades? How many of these techniques do you currently hear about today? The golf swing is simple, yet complex. When you play well everything seems so easy and then there are days where nothing works. I've heard you never own your golf swing, but you can rent it. Byron Nelson said "find a swing that works for you and spend the rest of your life trying to repeat it."

The reason for writing this story isn't to knock any golf instructor, but more for the student to understand everything they read or hear isn't necessarily the correct solution for their game. Personally, for my own knowledge and growth

I'll listen to many different theories on the golf swing. There are very few things more enjoyable for me than diving into golf swing theories. It's very important for me as an instructor to know what the best teachers in the world are teaching. When we stop trying to gain knowledge, we can find ourselves becoming stagnant and complacent with our instruction. Sometimes the hot player on tour will be working on a certain move that can complement your own game, but you should run it by your instructor before working hours on a new move on your own. It would most likely be a disaster if my student who is 74 years old and has two bad knees and limited flexibility tried to swing like Matt Wolff. Matt is an unbelievable player and should have great success on the PGA Tour, but not everyone can imitate his swing and have his success. Work with your instructor to find the swing you can consistently repeat and understand the new hot golf swing on tour might not be the cure for your own game. Spend time with your PGA Professional to help you find the correct swing cure for your game and spend a lifetime trying to repeat it!

CLARK GRISWOLD

We all have that person in our life who is negative about everything. In the movie Christmas Vacation Clark Griswold spent days hanging Christmas lights with multiple challenges. The entire movie theatre was laughing as Clark ran into challenge after challenge. When he finally got all the Christmas lights working, he brought the entire family out to admire the finished product. Each family member told him how beautiful the house looked while Clark had tears of joy running down his face. When it came time for his father-in-law to comment he said, "The lights aren't blinking." How many people have you played golf with who can't find anything good in their round? When you are in the golf business you hear the good and bad from your members coming off the course. There is a guy I've played at least eighty rounds with over the past twenty-five years and he fits the father-in-law description perfectly. It doesn't matter how perfect the day is he can still find something wrong. When I'm back in Fort Worth playing with him the comments and attitude are still the same. I absolutely love the guy, but when he gets to heaven he will probably complain about his mansion.

When you find the worst in everything you usually have more bad breaks because you actually expect the worst. We can't control bad breaks, but we can control how we handle bad breaks on the golf course. It amazes me to see how some people react to bad breaks on the course. Some people act like they are the only person to ever have their ball kick the wrong way or their putt does not break as they expected. When you play with people like this go ahead and press the bets because they are only going to compound the problem going forward in the round.

Chip Beck was Mr. Positive throughout his career, and he is one of the few to shoot 59 in a PGA Tour event. If he had a bad break, he didn't let it bother him and always tried to see the best in every situation. We have a saying in the

Professional Shop "It always works out." When my staff keeps this mindset, we maintain the attitude that no matter the challenge it will work out. I've preached this for sixteen years as Head Professional at Whispering Pines and anyone who works for me knows this is the way we approach every day.

We can all be the grumpy father-in-law in Christmas Vacation and notice the lights not blinking, or we can choose to see the best in everything rather than the worst. Take a Griswold approach to your golf game and enjoy your next round and don't worry about the Christmas lights not blinking!

COFFEE CAKE

Every Tuesday a group of men meet in the Elkins Lake locker room for a bible study. We started meeting in 2014 and use stories from my books and correlate them to a biblical application. I talk to the guys about the particular story we've chosen and the idea of how and why it was written. After my ten minutes of Q&A another gentlemen, who used to conduct bible studies at the pentagon, leads the bible study portion. It has been really cool to see how my stories that were written about golf can be used for a greater purpose.

This past Tuesday one of the guys brought his wife's famous coffee cake and before long the majority of the sweet goodness was gone. I'm not a big, sweet eater, but tried a piece and it was fantastic. As we sat there and discussed the chosen story for that particular week, it dawned on me that every single person was eating coffee cake. In a brief Segway I told the group they had just given me an idea for my next story.

If someone brought a great dessert every week, it would most certainly add a few pounds to all of us sitting around the table. It wouldn't be noticeable at first, but over the course of a few weeks or months it would be obvious our beltline would need to be loosened.

This is very similar to how bad habits creep into our golf swings. It isn't noticeable at first and our scores didn't change too much, but over time a bad swing habit can fester to the point where we are completely out of sorts with our game. Just like an innocent piece of pound cake each day can add weight to our bodies the golf swing can gradually get in bad positions. Nobody eats one piece of cake and it changes their weight overnight, but consistently doing this has a big effect. I've seen many students over the years that've put off taking a lesson until they are completely lost with their swing. Their alignment just a few yards off over time becomes twenty yards off. The over top move that was a slight pull has now become a big slice. These swing flaws crept into their game gradually and then became larger issues.

On the golf course don't wait until your overweight so to speak before changing the bad habit in your game. This

Christmas season think about working on your golf swing every time you see a dessert and your game could get better!

DON'T DOUBLE DOWN TO CATCH UP

One of my personal gambling rules when visiting Las Vegas is being disciplined regardless if the cards fall my way or I'm losing every bet. Double up to catch up is one way all the beautiful casinos get built in Sin City. The best gamblers continue the course and play mathematical odds without making emotional or spontaneous bets. On the golf course you see this all the time when the rounds not going your way and you try and force something to happen. Going for a sucker pin or charging a putt to try and make up for lost shots earlier in the round rarely works out. In golf just like in the casinos the breaks don't always fall your way. When the breaks aren't in your favor it's more advantageous to play conservative rather than double up on your bets to try and catch up. Charging that long putt when you should have lagged it close and secured a par is mathematically better for your score even if you three putted the previous hole. The undisciplined golfer runs the putt four feet past and misses the next one coming back. Your strategy shouldn't change based on good or bad breaks. You should have a disciplined approach and evaluate the consequences before hitting any shot. Stay consistent with your betting approach and use the same thought process on the golf course and you will shoot more consistent scores.

Don't Watch the Bad Stuff

Every year Riviera Country Club hosts a pro-am and invites many of the top clubs around the country. Whispering Pines is fortunate enough to get one of these invitations and my calendar is always marked for this great event. Not only is the golf course one of my favorite in the country; the event allows me to bring different members each year to experience Riviera. The pro-am is scheduled one week after the tour event and the course setup has the exact pins of the final round and the grandstands are still in place.

Having the ability to watch the final round of a PGA Tour event and then play the course eight days later should be an advantage. Watching the winner play the final holes should give you a blueprint on how you would like to play the hole during the pro-am. When we imprint good stuff, we tend to produce good stuff. Conversely, why would you want to watch sports center and see Ernie Els four-putt from three feet? We all get enamored with a train wreck and usually can't take our eyes off the television when it happens. The ending of Tin Cup made the movie famous and I'm sure you've played with someone who has quoted one of the lines from Kevin Costner's train wreck on the 72nd hole.

The mind is so powerful and watching or listening to anything that isn't making you better isn't worth putting into your thoughts. Garbage in always results in garbage out!

When we arrived Sunday, someone asked me about the melt down Ryan Palmer had on the 14th hole at Riviera. Obviously, you would wonder how a touring professional could make a nine on a par three. I'm sure he went back and forth in a few bunkers and most likely had a three putt. The truth is I've never watched it because it would only put a bad image in my mind about the hole. If you are asked not to think about an elephant, what is the natural reaction? You just thought of an elephant, didn't you? So why in the world would it benefit me to get to the 14th tee and think about how bad someone played the hole? It would be more beneficial to see someone making a hole in one and hit rewind a few times than to watch someone make a huge number on a hole we would play the following week.

When we arrived at the 14th tee my mind had no negative thoughts about what happened to Ryan Palmer. The wind was blowing in our face and it took a solid four iron to reach the left portion of the green. The undulating green made for a difficult two-putt, but my game managed to hold up and par the hole. I'm not six shots better than Ryan Palmer, but my score probably would have been higher if my curiosity got the best of me and I watched the replay.

When you watch the golf channel and you see someone having a Tin Cup moment, it's better to look away rather than watch the train wreck. If you ever get the chance to play Riviera think about my par on the 14th hole rather than Ryan

Palmer's nine and you will probably walk away with a good score.

DRUMBEAT

The difference in speed versus tempo is very similar to a drummer keeping a drumbeat. The drummer for a hard rock band, like Metallica, plays different than the drummer for George Strait. They both keep a consistent rhythm and tempo during each song, but their speed will differ. All golfers have a rhythm to their swing. Some of us have a Metallica type rhythm and some of us have a George Strait type rhythm. The key to both is having a consistent tempo!

EVH

Eddie Van Halen was my all-time favorite guitarist and this week's passing has saddened all of us who grew up loving VAN HALEN. Eddie was able to make the guitar sound different than anyone and thousands of guitarists followed in his footsteps trying to master his techniques. One of the unique technique's guitarist use is in the way they tune the guitar to create different sounds. Eddie Van Halen used this technique for the song unchained. Keith Richards would use different tuning for songs like Honky Tonk Women. If you are a Van Halen fan you know they had two completely different singers in David Lee Roth and Sammy Hagar. Sammy had a vocal range that is considered one of the best in rock music, where David Lee Roth had a limited range and is considered one of the best front men of all time. When DLR was the lead singer the tuning for Eddie Van Halen's guitar was tuned down to match the singers' vocal range. When Sammy was the lead singer Eddie would tune his guitar to a standard tuning because Sammy could hit all the notes. Ok.... you all are wondering how Eddie Van Halen tuning his guitar can help you with your golf game?

When you have a standard wedge shot into the green, but the wind is blowing 20 mph making a wedge to little club to reach your target you need to tune down. This would be an example of DLR not being able to hit the high notes unless

Eddie's guitar was tuned down. Tune down to an eight iron and you can reach your target when you don't have enough club due to the wind. When you have a perfect wedge distance with no wind you don't need to tune down, rather go ahead and hit your stock shot. Just like Sammy hitting those high notes in the song dreams.

The guitar has six strings that can be tuned numerous ways. The tuning should match the voice just like the club should match the distance. Sometimes you must adapt to make the shot fly the proper distance. Just like David Lee Roth would come up short hitting that vocal high note with standard tuning your shot would end up short trying to muscle that wedge into a 20-mph breeze.

When the winds not blowing use your standard tuning and hit the stock shot like Sammy Hagar. When the wind is blowing adapt like David Lee Roth has to do with tuning down the guitar to match his voice.

Next time you tee up crank up some VAN HALEN and remember when it's windy listen to Diamond Dave and when it's not windy listen to the Red Rocker. Both made incredible music doing it different ways and so can you on the golf course!

RIP EVH

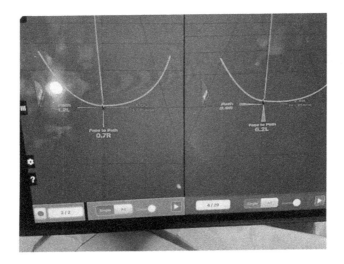

Here is an example of how two separate golf shots ended up in the same place and same distance with totally different path and face data.

Screen left my path was 1.2 to the left with 0.7 face with a total of 1.9

Screen right my path was 8.9 to the right with 6.2 closed face with a total 15.10

When you combine the two numbers of a shot and the combined amount is less than 4 you are playing in the area of consistent golf.

When your numbers combined are above 4 you need more timing and it's much harder to consistently repeat.

Perfection is 0.0 path and 0.0 face

Swing Path + Face to Path = 4 or less for great golf

This is the formula used for all my students!

The data we are able to use today helps the teacher teach better and the students learn faster.

FORGET THE BAD ROUND

One of the outstanding collegiate players, who plays at Whispering Pines periodically, mentioned to me a dilemma he was having with his coach. His coach asked him to fill out a report card, so to speak, of his round. This is something the coach asks of his players so they can evaluate their performance, along with the coach evaluating the player's performance. The collegiate player was adamant about not doing this for his coach because it was his last round of the season and it happened to be a bad round that happened on national television in the NCAA Championship. I told him he should do what his coach asked and why was it such a big deal. The collegiate player told me he was frustrated about his performance and basically wanted to forget about it entirely. He said when he plays a bad round, he doesn't want to ever think about it again and especially have to go through his scorecard again and relive it.

This was interesting to me because this player is one of the top amateurs in the country and his mindset was entirely different than the rest of us playing this game. Most of my students, along with myself, tend to go over each bad shot replaying it over and over in our mind. This tends to carry over to the next round and the downward spiral starts in our game. Great players let it go and don't rehash the bad shots.

Rather than obsessing about how bad they played they tend to think the bad round was a fluke and will not happen again.

I'm not saying you shouldn't go through your round and look at ways to improve, but don't let your bad round eat away at the progress you've made in your game. Nobody plays great golf all the time and tournament players lose more than they ever win.

This collegiate player will be on the PGA Tour in a few years and showed me how great players think about bad rounds. Forget your last bad round and focus on your next great round. Remember the windshield in your car is bigger than the rearview mirror for a reason.

GOING BACK TO THE EX-GIRLFRIEND

We've all done it and usually regretted the decision to go back to the ex-girlfriend. How many of you have done the same thing in your golf game? Your pro gives you the perfect relationship advice for your golf swing and you completely buy into the change. It is so uncomfortable, but you promised yourself you would stick to the plan for the new and improved swing. After a few rounds you decide it's too uncomfortable and you go back to your old swing. This is like going through a breakup and never seeing the possibility of someone coming into your life who could be as good as what you had. If you go back to the ex-girlfriend, you might have missed out on the person of your dreams coming into your life. Sometimes we hold onto things we should let go of to be able to grow in areas of our lives.

The number of times a student goes back to their old swing only to find they continue to have the same outcome is maddening. It's always more comfortable to stick with the old golf swing, but don't plan to have different results if you choose this route. Going through a painful divorce and never seeing the possibility of being happy again is something many of us have gone through in life. When you finally come out on the other side and find someone who completes your life it is easier to look back and see how much better life can be with this new person. No doubt there is plenty of pain involved, but the end-result is rewarding. If you knew you could be a better golfer, but you had to shoot some bad rounds and hit some embarrassing shots during the process would you do it? Getting better sometimes involves tough changes and many hours of time to achieve the game you want. If you want to play the best golf of your life you might have to give up on the old golf swing and build a new relationship with your new swing!

HANGING WITH AN AGGIE LEGEND

One of the greatest parts about my job is all the great people you meet. Golf brings people together from all walks of life. It does not matter if you are a professional athlete, musician, or a political figure they all are golfers when they come through the gates at Whispering Pines.

Recently, RC Slocum asked me to play golf with his group at Traditions Club, in College Station. Coach Slocum has been to Whispering Pines a few times and have had the pleasure to get to know him a little bit.

Coach Slocum is the winningest Texas A&M football coach in the history of the program. I am an Oklahoma

Sooner fan and will always root for Oklahoma but dating a girl who proudly wears her aggie ring and spending time with coach makes them my favorite *other* team.

We had a great day on the course with lots of wonderful stories about coaching and big games played at Kyle Field. When we finished the round, we had a coke and talked about golf swings and my teaching philosophies. Golfers are like fisherman and really perk up when they hear someone talking about how to perform better at their sport. Coach Slocum seemed intrigued as my swing theories were unveiled on the patio and later that week called and asked for a lesson.

A few months later, Coach Slocum, asked me and my girlfriend to meet he and his wife for the weekend in Carmel, California. My girlfriend was so excited, not only to go to Pebble Beach and get out of the Texas heat, but to spend time with the Head Football Coach when she attended A&M. My joke to her the entire week was *you are hanging out with an A&M legend and cannot even arrange a dinner for me and Coach Switzer*. Spending time with Coach Slocum was a wonderful opportunity to ask questions about all the things you ever wanted to know about college football. The number of stories he told on the golf course or at the house in the morning drinking coffee were all priceless. It was a weekend where you wish you had a tape recorder to record every incredible story.

Our last day we were scheduled to play The Preserve Golf Club up in the mountains of Carmel Valley. When you arrive at the gate the clubhouse is still another 25 minutes along a winding road up the mountain. The question that was most intriguing to me was if there was ever a game where the coaching staff did not know how to counter what the other team was doing. Specifically, my question was related to OU playing A&M in the Cotton Bowl and OU getting dismantled by Johnny Manziel. Even though Coach Slocum wasn't the coach for that game I knew he would have insight. As we drove up the winding mountain road, he told me there was not a game that the team and coaches were not prepared for whatever they might face. Sometimes they might not execute well enough to win, but they were always prepared for any situation.

The typical golfer hits shots on the range from a perfect lie with the same club usually not aiming at a specific target. Short game practice is usually hitting a few chips from a perfect lie with the same club. What happens when you get on the course and your ball is in the rough or on a sidehill lie? If you only practice perfect situations it would be the same a Coach Slocum practicing as if the defense would never tackle his offensive players and the safety would intercept every pass thrown in the game. This is not realistic in football and getting a perfect lie every time, you reach your ball is not realistic either. When you get to the driving range work on shots you will have during your round. Practice

35

hitting shots from different lies and angles. When I am working with students, I will take them to a downslope off the side of the tee box and have them hit shots and then take them to a side slope and hit shots. The student can see how the ball reacts and adjust. When you work on your short game do not hit balls from the exact spot over and over. You are not getting better practicing like this! Create different lies around the green, hit bunker shots from buried lies, sidehill lies etc. When you practice with the expectation of something could go wrong you will be prepared when it happens.

Coach Slocum and his wife were the perfect hosts, and we were honored to be able to spend time with them for the weekend. The stories Coach Slocum told could fill three books and they would all be best sellers. The knowledge he has is incredible, but more than that he is an unbelievable person. The integrity he has and the grace he has shown impressed me more than any big game won at Kyle Field. If he were still coaching for the aggies and my son wanted to play football my choice would be for my kid to play for him.

Prepare for everything that could happen in your next round of golf and you will not be surprised if your ball happens to find a not so perfect lie.

GIG EM

HOGAN HITTING OFF THE DECK

Many years ago, a great golf professional by the name of Roland Harper was the teaching pro at Colonial Country Club in Fort Worth. Before he became the teaching professional, he was the head golf professional for thirty-one years at this historic club. I used to have lunch with him at least once every few weeks and pick his brain as a young twenty-four-year-old assistant. Roland was respected among all the membership and to this day when his name is mentioned to people who knew him, they always have something very nice to say. Roland would always take time out of his practice session to work with me on my golf swing or answer questions about teaching. Over the years it was a blessing to get to talk to someone with so much knowledge that was willing to share their ideas about the golf swing and the club business.

Roland had so many Hogan stories and actually played with him the last round he would ever play at the course where he won five times. He told this story to me one day while we were eating lunch in the 19th Hole. He said, like most everyone I've ever talked to about Mr. Hogan, you didn't talk unless he talked to you first. There was certainly a reverence when you were in the presence of this legend according to Roland. The last day they played together, Roland said Mr. Hogan flinched a bit on his tee shot on the par three fourth hole. Nobody in the group said anything, but everyone knew something wasn't right after that shot. They continued to play with nobody saying anything when they reached the par three eighth hole. Roland said Mr. Hogan flinched on the tee shot with a grimace on his face and told the group *"that's all today guys "*and walked back to the clubhouse. Nobody knew at that point this would be the last round he would ever play at Colonial.

Another great story Roland told me was the day a board member called and said, *"Hogan is practicing on the golf course and needs to be told he can't practice."* Roland said the last thing he wanted to do is tell Ben Hogan to get off the course with his shag bag. He knew he had to go out and talk to Mr. Hogan because he was the head professional, and a board member was requesting this to be handled. Roland drove out to hole fourteen and there was the hawk hitting four woods off the tee, just like the member said. Roland kept his distance and noticed Mr. Hogan was hitting every shot perfect without disturbing a blade of grass. There were no divots anywhere on the tee box as each ball was striped with precision down the fairway. I asked Roland what he said, and he smiled and said, *"I turned the cart the opposite direction and went back to the golf shop."*

The most important thing Roland ever told me was the day I asked him *"How did you keep your job over thirty years at such a demanding, high profile, country club?"* He looked me directly in the eyes and said, *"Chris if you always treat everyone equal and never play favorites with the membership you will never have to worry about someone getting on the board and getting you fired."* I've tried to live by his words of wisdom my entire golf career. We all have members we enjoy more than others, but every member should feel like they are the most important member when they walk in the professional shop.

Roland passed many years ago from a long battle with cancer. He was a great man and my time spent with him in the nineteenth hole were some of the best life lessons a young assistant pro could ever have. When you have the opportunity to spend time with someone who has been on this earth much longer than you, use that time to pick their brain and gain as much knowledge as you can. His words of wisdom have definitely helped me in my career in the golf industry.

HOLD ON LOOSELY

This weekend, while giving a lesson; I put my hands on the student's club to adjust their grip. The tension was so tight that it was difficult to even move their hands. The obvious question was asked from their golf professional, "Why are you holding on so tight?" If you were ever crazy enough to ride a bull it would be advantageous to hang on very tight, but you're holding onto a golf club.

When you grip a golf club tight it creates tension throughout your arms and chest. On a scale from one to ten your grip pressure should be about a four. The great Sam Sneed used to tell students to hold the club like they would hold a small bird in their hands. You want to hold tight enough where the bird couldn't fly away, but not too tight as to harm it. I tell my students to hold the grip like a tube of toothpaste with the cap off and squeeze only hard enough to put a small amount on your toothbrush. Both these examples make the point of having light grip pressure.

Light grip pressure on a full swing gives you more speed and increased distance. Try to hit a driver squeezing as hard as you can and then hit a shot with light grip pressure and see which shot goes farther. When you putt with light grip pressure this allows you to feel the club head better and frees up your stroke. Great putters hold the club with very little tension in their arms or hands. Loosen up your grip in all areas and you will play better golf!

Hold on loosely and don't let go. If you cling too tightly you're going to lose control. Who knew 38 Special was writing a song about golf!

HOW TO PLAY A TOURNAMENT PRACTICE ROUND

In 2004 one of my students went through all three stages of PGA Qualifying School. Walking the courses during those practice rounds were some of the best coaching moments of my life. I'll never forget when my student hit a five iron for his second shot on a par five to six feet from the hole. If you have an eagle putt you definitely want to make it, but my student walked over to his ball and picked it up and started hitting putts to where he thought the hole would be during the tournament. This impressed me so much because the putt meant nothing to him during a practice round. If he did putt it in for an eagle and then made par during the tournament round, he would have felt like he lost two strokes. Every hole was dissected from tee to green and a strategy was formed on exactly how to play each hole. When he putted out on his 90th hole at Orange County National he had earned his PGA Tour card.

The weather also plays into how you play your practice round. My last collegiate tournament practice round the weather was spectacular. The next morning when we left our hotel for the golf course the weather had changed in a big way. The wind was blowing out of the north at 30mph and the temperature had dropped thirty degrees from the previous day. All the shots we had played in the practice round would be played completely different in the tournament round.

When you prepare for tournament you should always check the weather forecast and play your practice round keeping in mind the wind conditions you might expect. The Open is a great example of drastic weather changes and the golf course playing completely different from one day to the next. When the best players in the world prepare for The Open, they play practice rounds at different times of the day, so they get both types of weather. The wind usually picks up as the day goes on and the morning guys historically have it easier than the afternoon groups. If you played every practice round in the morning you would be in for a rough afternoon for one of the rounds.

When the PGA Tour would come to Fort Worth it was more enjoyable for me to watch the guys play their practice rounds than to watch the tournament. Nick Faldo was playing a late practice round and I just happened to catch him play the ninth hole at Colonial Country Club as the sun was beginning to set. Nick teed off and purposely hit one tee shot to the right side of the fairway, one shot to the left side of the fairway and one in the center of the fairway. His strategy was to play different tee shots based on where the pin might be in the tournament rounds. The coolest part of this story is he decided not to hit the ball on the left side of the fairway and asked me to throw him his golf ball. Reaching down to pick up his precept golf ball he immediately went into a batter's stance like he was playing for the LA Dodgers. I threw the ball thirty yards to him and he made a swing and a miss and waved to me saying thank you in his English accent.

The rough and sand should always be tested during a practice round even if you think you will hit every green and fairway. Throwing a few balls in the rough around the green to see how the ball reacts will be advantageous if you don't have your best ball striking day and find yourself in the greenside rough. Hitting some shots from greenside bunker with different lies to see how ball reacts is also very important. Bunker sand and how they are manicured are different from course to course. The bunkers at Whispering Pines are compacted and firm where some courses have heavier sand and play completely different. You want to be prepared for the different shots around the green you might encounter during your tournament. When you practice like this there will not be any surprises when the tournament starts.

Last of all and most important in playing a practice round is spending plenty of time on the greens. When you go to Augusta and watch the guys play their practice rounds, they spend an enormous amount of time on the greens. All the guys now have books with that show the contours of the greens. You never see a PGA Tour player not looking at his green chart book these days. The amount of information gathered in a practice round can really make a difference in how you ultimately play in the tournament. If you prepare properly in the practice round your chance of success will increase. If you go out and try and shoot your best score ever during a practice round, you probably won't win the event.

Remember, practice rounds are for practice not score!

THE BOOK

If you have been to Las Vegas and played blackjack you have heard the dealer say, "The book says." What the dealer means is the book that the casinos print out tell you what you should do in this game based on the cards you have and the cards the dealer is showing. The book isn't fool proof because the casinos wouldn't give you this information if it created winners, but it is helpful when making decisions on the blackjack table. The yardage book does the same for the golfer playing the course. The yardage book gives specific information on distance to bunkers from different tee boxes along with slopes on the greens. Obviously if you have a yardage book it doesn't guarantee lower scores, but it definitely gives you good information to make educated decisions for each shot.

Wouldn't it be great if there was a book for each golf course that told you what play you should make on each shot? If you are in the trees and have three options and the book says pitch out sideways, punchout down the fairway, or split the gap between the trees and go for it. Unfortunately, there isn't a book for these situations, but you can put past outcomes from these types of situations in your own book. When you finish a round of golf write in a log about your round and what you could have done better to shoot a lower score. The book in Vegas gives you the best advice based on percentages with no guarantee of the outcome. You should approach every shot going through your percentage checklist. Would your book say to hit the low percentage shot and risk making a big number or pitch-out with the safe shot and hope the dealer busts? You should never split kings and you should never try a shot you know you can't pull off. Splitting two aces makes sense in blackjack but splitting two trees sometimes will make you bust!

THE JACKET

One of my young junior players named Cash was taking a lesson last October. The weather had just turned cool enough to wear a jacket and we happened to just get a shipment of KJUS jackets in that week. I personally cannot stand the heat and always look forward to the first day of Fall when it is cool enough to wear a jacket on the course. Cash arrived for his lesson and immediately told me how much he liked my new jacket. Cash is a very good player and will play college golf without a doubt. He is extremely long off the tee and has a short game to match. We went through a session in the teaching facility getting his numbers on Trackman along with some video work to tighten up his mechanics. After working on full swing, we went out to the needler par three course to work on his wedge shots and putting. The needler is a magical place to work on all aspects of your game. A few years ago, Lee Trevino came to Whispering Pines and I was fortunate enough to play with him on the big course and then the needler to close out an unforgettable day. When Lee had played a few of the holes on the needler he stopped and told me he would join this course just to be able to practice on the needler. What a compliment from one of the legends of the game! I jokingly mentioned he could fill out a membership application and he would have no problem becoming a member. All this to say you can hit every shot imaginable on the needler and it is the best place to take students to work on different parts of their game.

Often, with my students, I will challenge them with a certain part of their game and attach a prize if they can perform the task. Sometimes the prize will be a discounted lesson or buying them a hat from the professional shop. Cash was preparing for an upcoming tournament, so the challenge was made that he had to hole a twenty-foot putt and the prize was a new KJUS jacket. When the challenge was made his eyes lit up a bit along with a big smile. He lined up the putt and confidently rolled it in and immediately told me I did not have to buy him a jacket. KJUS jackets are very expensive and even with my discount it cost me my hourly rate. Buying him the jacket made me just as happy as Cash making the putt to win it. Every time he wears that jacket, he knows he earned it. Every time he has a twenty-foot putt to win a tournament he can draw off that moment where he beat his instructor out of a jacket. When you practice put something on the line before you leave the range or putting green. You might bet yourself something like not having a cup of coffee for a week if you don't make the putt or reward yourself if there is something you have been wanting to purchase if you pull off the shot. When we challenge ourselves with a prize attached our intensity level goes up. If we practiced like there was a prize attached to the outcome we would perform better on the course. Most of us work on our chipping without thinking about holing the shot, but what if every shot hit was 100% committed to holing the shot. You might not hole any of the shots, but your proximity to the hole would be much closer if you tried to hole the shot rather than just get it close.

Cash might have made the putt without having a prize attached, but his intensity went up a level when he knew there would be a reward. Practice like you want to play and you will play like you practice! The moral to this story is never bet a kid with a name like CASH and think he is not going to win the money!

THE OPENING TEE SHOT

Technically this is the most nerve-racking shot in the game. Even the best players in the world get nervous when teeing up their first shot of the day. Working as a PGA Professional for the past 28 years I've watched tens of thousands of players tee off in the member guest or club championship. It's interesting to see how ultra-successful businessmen and former professional athletes can get so nervous hitting their first tee shot. I've played with hall of fame basketball and football players and they all stepped up to the first tee with butterflies in their stomach and shaky hands. These are players who were MVP of Super Bowls and NBA Champions. They've hit winning shots on the court and made touchdowns for their teams in the biggest games of their lives. I've played with musicians who stand on a stage and perform their music to tens of thousands of fans every night and they get just as nervous as my 15-handicap member.

So why would anyone get nervous when they've accomplished so much in their chosen professions? The reason it's just you and that golf ball sitting on a peg in the ground and everyone in your group watching as you make your first swing. I've been there before and have hit some interesting tee-shots in my life. I've had nightmares the night before a tournament round and woken up with anxiety. The main thing to understand, when standing on the first tee, is everyone feels just like you. Jack Nicklaus said if he wasn't nervous over his first tee shot then the round didn't mean much. Hank Haney described Tiger Woods walking from the range after an incredible warm-up, hitting some of the ugliest tee shots on the first hole you've ever seen. So, if the two greatest golfers who've every played the game struggle with nerves on the first tee shouldn't we feel the same?

The worst tee shot of my life was a few years ago at the Cabo Pro-Am. My first round had been good and my warm-up session before the start of the second round was great. My pro-am team all hit good tee shots off the first hole on the desert course and Cabo Del Sol. I walked up to the tee joking with my guys and full of confidence for what the day was going to bring. The first hole on the desert course is adjacent to the range and putting green and is a slight dogleg left par four. I've hit numerous tee shots over the years, some good and some bad, but nothing like this shot. Do you remember the huge boulder at the TPC Stadium course in Arizona that the fans moved so Tiger Woods would have an unobstructed shot? I swear they moved it right in front of the first tee at the desert course at Cabo Del Sol. On any course in the world the tee shot I hit that morning would have been a low screamer that would roll out 280 yards. It wouldn't have been pretty, but it would have been in the center of the fairway. The Tiger Woods boulder, sixty yards off the tee and directly in my line, was just a bit too big for my heeled driver to clear that day. Holding my pos and watching my ball ricochet backwards, flying over my head and landing somewhere by the clubhouse one hundred yards behind me was embarrassing. The worst part was seeing my members out of my peripheral and seeing their eyes tracking my ball flying backwards. What do you say after the most embarrassing tee shot of your life? I looked at the tournament staff standing directly behind me and smile at them and said, "I bet you haven't seen a tee shot like that one before?" I teed up another ball and striped it down the fairways and told the tournament staff "This is going to be the best bogey of the tournament." The next day for the final round we were playing the ocean course. The tournament staff all were quiet when I approached the tee and the elephant in the room was obviously my tee shot heard around the Baja Peninsula from the previous day. I smiled at the staff and said, "I noticed there isn't a hug boulder in my line for this opening tee shot." Everyone laughed at the comment and then hit the best tee shot of the week in front of my team and the tournament staff.

My tee shot hitting the boulder could have ruined my round and the rest of the tournament, but that would only happen if I allowed it. Instead of being humiliated I laughed it off, because that one shot didn't define me, nor did it keep me from playing a solid round. The next day at the ocean course I knew regardless of how my tee shot was hit it would never be as bad as the day before. If you hit the best tee shot of your life chalk it up as a great start and birdie the hole! If you hit the worst shot of your life take the mind-set of how great a par, you are going to make and plan on playing great the rest of the day!

Here are a few ways to help with the opening tee-shot for your next tournament round or Saturday match at the country club.

• Breath deep and let as much air out of your lungs to release tension

• Grip the club light as we tend to tighten your grip when feeling pressure

• Slow down and have good rhythm as we usually speed up our tempo

• Visualize the shot you want to hit

• Don't leave the range until you have hit the exact shot you are trying to hit on the first tee.

• Keep in mind it is only a game and it is only one shot! This shot doesn't determine how good of a

person you are, how good you are in business, or define your golf game.

THE PESSIMISTIC GOLFER

When you are pessimistic about something happening and it actually happens you experience the bad thing twice. Optimistic people think about the best outcome and if it doesn't happen, they only have to experience the bad thing once.

Let's put this in golf terms on how the pessimistic person thinks about their game. The pessimist golfer thinks he is going to play bad, expects to play bad, and usually plays bad. If the pessimist plays a good round, they usually talk about the bad things in the round even though they scored well.

The optimist golfer can find the good in their round even when it's not their best day on the links. They shoot a bad score but tell you they putted well. They hit a drive out of bounds and tell you how solid they struck the shot. These types of people see the best in everything and most of time are happier people in life.

We all have the friend we can call up and they put a smile on our face within the first minute of the conversation. One of my best friends on the planet, who lives in Arlington, can have me laughing and smiling whenever he calls. He sees the best in every situation and anyone who knows him loves being around him. This week my sister called and asked me a question about something she was wanting do with her family. When she heard my answer, she said "That's why I called you and not your brother because you see the positive in everything." That's a nice compliment coming from my sister, but that is truly how I try to live my life.

Bruce Edwards caddied for Tom Watson for the majority of his career. For a short time he caddied for Greg Norman when he was the #1 player in the world. One day someone asked him what the difference was caddying for two of the greats in golf. Bruce said if Greg Norman found his ball in a divot in the fairway, he would get angry and frustrated that the divot wasn't replaced by the person who hit the shot before him. Bruce said when Tom Watson found his ball in a divot in the fairway he would say "Watch how good this shot is going to be!"

We've got a short time on this earth and we can't determine what happens to us through this journey, but we do determine how we react!

THE TALE OF TWO IRISH MEN

The British Open returned to Ireland this year and one of the favorites to win golf's oldest championship was Rory McIlroy. Rory has been one of the top players in the world since he came onto the PGA Tour. He's won every major except the Masters as I'm writing this and seemed to be destined to possibly challenge Tiger Woods record in majors. Shane Lowry has been a good player for a long-time as well but has never been considered someone who could challenge Rory on a career basis. All of Ireland was cheering for their countrymen to play well and hopefully bring the claret jug to a pub in Northern Ireland on Sunday evening of golf greatest major. Rory was a heavy favorite to win the tournament months before and had been in great form all year. Shane Lowry has had a good career, but with no disrespect not even close to Rory's career accomplishments.

After all the build-up, practice rounds, and press conferences being asked what it would mean to win the British Open in your home country Rory arrived at the first tee. With the crowd cheering his name with thunderous applause, Rory pulled a long iron shot out of bounds. As the crowd gasped in unbelief Rory proceeded to make a quadruple eight on the first hole in route to a 79 first round score. Shane Lowry on the other hand opened with a 67 clipping the most famous Irishman by 12 shots.

It's extremely difficult to win a PGA Tour event when the event is played in your hometown. Living in Fort Worth for ten years there were plenty of tour players in the DFW area who played the Byron Nelson and the Colonial. Spieth won the Colonial, but he's from Dallas and Rory Sabatini won the Byron Nelson, but lives in Fort Worth and originally from South Africa. We all know Ben Hogan won Colonial five times with Fort Worth being his hometown, but winning in your home town doesn't happen often. Now think about your entire country cheering for you along with being the favorite to win the event. How much pressure can you put on a golfer in a major championship? In my opinion this would be even more difficult than playing in a Ryder Cup in your home European country. In a Ryder Cup you have a team to fall back on if you're not playing your best. In the 148th British Open it's just you against the field. Of course, there were other Irish players in the event besides Rory, but nobody had the credentials and fire power of McIlroy coming into this event.

Rory during his practice round hit a shot out of bounds to the right on the starting hole. On Thursday Rory pulled his tee shot badly to the left out of bounds on the starting hole. It would be interesting to ask Rory if he was thinking about the out of bounds on the right as he stood over the first tee shot of his opening round. If you are telling yourself don't hit the ball to the right two things usually happen. You either hit the ball to the right, *self- fulfilling prophecy,* or you hit the ball as far left as possible to avoid the shot you do not want to hit. Secondly, putting pressure on yourself to play well rarely produces great results. We've seen Phil Mickelson every year trying his best to win the US OPEN, his only major left to complete the grand slam of golf. We will see this with Jordan Spieth for many years at the PGA Championship until he finally wins one. When you want something too much it rarely works out and when it finally does you usually were able to downplay the moment to some extent. I'm not saying Shane Lowry didn't care, but he was able to control his nerves and stay in the moment better than the other Irishmen playing in the event. Rory followed his 79 with a blistering

65 the next day and unfortunately missed the cut. Rory's score on Friday even though 14 shots better doesn't mean he found something magical in his swing 24 hours later. This is the same person who shot the course record 61 at the same course when he was a teenager. I bet his mindset when he shot the 61 and the tournament round of 65 were probably very close to the same. His mindset when he shot the 79 was probably an out of body experience, which we've all had if you've played this game long enough. Rory made the moment bigger than it needed to be with his horrific start when he should have been in contention on Sunday.

The tale of the two Irishmen is simple. Both wanted to win, both prepared well, both tried very hard, but only one handled his nerves and the moment well enough to win in his home country. If you have a club championship coming up or a big event at your home club remember this year's British Open. You can want something too bad and it could actually back-fire. Prepare your best and get your mind in a good place. Picture yourself winning the tournament weeks before and see yourself holding the trophy.

Shane Lowry probably did all of these things in the 148th Open and you can too!

THE THINGS YOU NOTICE

Isn't it funny the things you notice when someone points it out to you? How about the person who says "you know" to start every sentence? You have never noticed this, but someone pointed it out to you and now you count the number of times the person says "you know" in every conversation. We all have our little quirks and I've got plenty so no judgement coming from me in this story. I'm currently in the process of building a new home and trying to choose the type of stone that would look best. The amount of stone to choose from is mind-numbing. The number of houses I've driven by to find the best stone has been nauseating. It has become impossible for me to drive anywhere and not notice the stone on every house and building. It's even gotten to the point where I caught myself admiring the stonework at Chick-fil-a yesterday!

All of you who have taken lessons have had your instructor give you some drill to work on in your swing. The instructor will usually pull up a PGA Tour player and show you an example of how they perform the move they are trying to incorporate in your swing. You might need to turn your hips faster, shallow the shaft, or have more forward shaft lean. We all have things we can improve in our swings and a good instructor can identify this. Once you know your move start watching the guys on the PGA Tour broadcast and really focus on that one thing. You might not have ever noticed how frequently you see Tiger, Rory or Jordon make this move in their own swings until it was mentioned to you by your instructor. Just like my quest for the perfect stone to go on my new house or the annoying quirk someone might say, once you've noticed this you will notice all the time. Take this OCD approach and put it to good use in your own game. Ask you instructor what to look for in the professional's swing that you can emulate and eventually incorporate in your own swing. Once you've been made aware you will start looking at that one thing in your swing like I'm looking at the stone on every home and building!

Tournament Golf

PGA Golf Professionals are not professional golfers and play much less than most people would think. Working at Whispering Pines is one of the best places in the country to be the golf professional for many reasons. My typical day involves meeting and greeting our members and their guests, giving swing tips on the range, merchandising the professional shop, running our tournaments, checking on pace of play and the list goes on. Most people tend to think my job only involves playing golf and assume my clubs are being used every day. The typical PGA Golf Professional plays maybe fifty full rounds of golf per year. When I worked at Colonial the golf pros actually kept their handicaps, another myth that all of us are scratch or better, along with tracking our total rounds. The most I ever played topped out at thirty-two rounds as an assistant professional. Teaching and taking care of the membership always takes precedence over my game.

The bulk of my rounds usually happen in the off-season when our club is closed. This is the time where we take member trips and pro-am tournaments around the country. This is the only time my clubs go on the links three days in a row. These trips create friendships and allow me to get to know our members on a more personal level. I'm a huge believer that every PGA Professional should make time to spend with their members away from the club on golf trips a few times per year. The past few weeks I've taken different members to some wonderful courses around the country along with visiting members at their home clubs in Texas. Like previously mentioned my game travels to a three handicap, not scratch, the majority of the year. The past few months the golf game has been better than usual, and my scores have reflected this. The courses where these scores were shot will not be mentioned, but they were all exceptional facilities with the majority being famous courses we've all heard of. All of the scores listed are rounds played with members in a relaxed environment and one of the scores is an individual tournament round. The scores are in numerical order as they were shot 74-72-71-81-76-74-75-72. Can you guess the tournament score?

Tournament golf is different than golf with your buddies and the 81 is proof. Putting out every three-foot putt and knowing your score will be posted on a scoreboard creates a different kind of pressure than your Saturday foursome with your friends. After the tournament round it's typical for me to beat myself up and go over every shot. My mindset was in a good place that morning before the event, my scores leading up to the event had given me confidence, and there was no reason to think my round wouldn't be good. The smallest bit of pressure makes most of us speed up our tempo and typically grip the club tighter, creating tension throughout the body. When you hear people talk about feeling like they had an out-of-body experience on the golf course this is what they mean.

After processing this for a few days and then playing some really good rounds after the tournament I realized my total individual tournament rounds in a calendar year equate to maybe five rounds. This equates to 10% of my total golf rounds played in an average year. How can anyone expect to play great and deal with the pressure of a tournament round when 90% of their rounds are played in a relaxed environment with their friends? PGA Tour guys play one or two practice rounds, one pro-am, and four tournament rounds if they make the cut every week. Phil Mickelson mentioned in an interview it takes him at least three tournaments in the beginning of the season to feel comfortable. If a Hall of Fame golfer needs twelve tournament rounds to get rid of the butterflies how can we expect to manage our tournament rounds when the only tournament round most people play is their club championship.

So how do we get better playing in tournaments? You have to play more tournaments or simulate a tournament atmosphere when you play at your home club. Having to post your score and putt everything out is a great start. No more giving putts from three feet and taking mulligans off the first tee if you want to be a successful tournament player. It's no surprise our club champion at Whispering Pines plays in other tournaments throughout the year on a regular basis and played competitively the past forty years.

There is nothing wrong with playing golf with your buddies and enjoying the casual round, but the tournament golfer needs to put something on the line every time they tee it up. I'm working on being a better tournament player and posting the 81 is embarrassing, but it's part of the process.

The next time you tee it up don't take a mulligan, hole out every putt, count every shot and simulate what you might feel the next time you register for your club championship.

TRACKMAN				PGA TOUR AVERAGES				WWW.TRACKMANGOLF.COM
	Club Speed (mph)	Attack Angle (deg)	Ball Speed (mph)	Smash Factor	Launch Ang. (deg)	Spin Rate (rpm)	Max Height (yds)	Land Angle (deg)	Carry (yds)
Driver	113	-1.3°	167	1.48	10.9°	2686	32	38°	275
3-wood	107	-2.9°	158	1.48	9.2°	3655	30	43°	243
5-wood	103	-3.3°	152	1.47	9.4°	4350	31	47°	230
Hybrid 15-18°	100	-3.5°	146	1.46	10.2°	4437	29	47°	225
3 Iron	98	-3.1°	142	1.45	10.4°	4630	27	46°	212
4 Iron	96	-3.4°	137	1.43	11.0°	4836	28	48°	203
5 Iron	94	-3.7°	132	1.41	12.1°	5361	31	49°	194
6 Iron	92	-4.1°	127	1.38	14.1°	6231	30	50°	183
7 Iron	90	-4.3°	120	1.33	16.3°	7097	32	50°	172
8 Iron	87	-4.5°	115	1.32	18.1°	7998	31	50°	160
9 Iron	85	-4.7°	109	1.28	20.4°	8647	30	51°	148
PW	83	-5.0°	102	1.23	24.2°	9304	29	52°	136

We all watch the guys on the PGA Tour hit the ball forever. Take a look at these numbers and understand the averages are much different than what you see on television each week. The guys you watch playing in the final few groups are playing the best golf of their season and their adrenaline is full throttle. PGA Tour course setups have the fairways rolling about 10 on a stimp meter. My club head speed with a driver is around 109 and my average drive is 285 total yards. When the average tour player carries the ball 275, they are usually getting 30 plus yards of roll. Keep these numbers in mind the next time you start getting down on yourself after seeing Rory hit a 196-yard eight iron!

TRACKMAN AND FLIGHT SCOPE

Trackman and flight scope are like an MRI for a golfer. Get the information and then turn it off. They don't continue to put you in and out of the MRI machine when you have to get one. Once you come out of the machine, they have the images needed and give to the doctor to read.

Too many teachers continue to put their students back and forth in the machine so to speak. Trying to get perfect numbers leads a lot of students down the path of playing swing rather than playing golf. I'll use this technology for a few minutes, find the consistent issue and then turn it off. The technology makes us better and faster at analyzing the swing, but we are still the doctor who has to teach the student not the machine.

TV GUIDE

Most people under the age of forty have no idea what a paper tv guide looks like. We used to have to look at our weekly or monthly television guidebook to see when our favorite shows would air. We also did not have remote controls and had to physically walk to the television and manually turn a knob to change the channel.

My girlfriend has two remote controls for the living room television. The smaller remote was used for changing the channel and the volume and the larger remote was for turning on the guide for easier access finding the stations. I've watched television at her house going on six years now and never once did we watch television without using both remotes. The other night, while using the smaller remote, which has no button saying guide, I pressed the right corner in the middle of the controller and the guide appeared on the television screen. This was a eureka moment for everyone watching knowing this had happened with the smaller remote. My girlfriend's son asked me how I had turned on the guide without having the larger remote control. Smiling with a smirk of pride I showed him how to do what had never been done in the history of this remote control.

This was a total accident, and everyone knew that I had stumbled on this newfound way to turn on the guide and essentially get rid of the big remote. This is exactly what many of us have done on the driving range after hitting hundreds of balls and then hitting that perfect shot. The difference with most of us after hitting our perfect shot we do not stop to think about how we accomplished the perfect shot. Just like the remote-control moment if I had not stopped to figure out what had happened, we would have kept using the two-remote system. It would have been easy to keep watching television and never try to figure out why the guide turned on, but instead pressing the button again to confirm this was the correct way to turn on the guide created the new one-remote system. I have had this happen to me on many occasions whether it was working on my short-game or hitting balls on the range. We have all heard of PGA Tour players saying they found something during a practice session. Tiger Woods famously called his swing coach from the range one evening and said he found it. After that call to his coach Tiger went on a streak like nobody has ever seen in golf. What if Tiger would have raked another ball over and hit another shot on the range without stopping to think about what he had just done? There are little moments we all have that teach us life lessons and golf lessons, but it is our job to stop and think about what lesson was learned and apply it.

Now that I'm thinking about it, I was the remote control for my dad growing up!

WATCHING GREAT GOLF AND PLAYING GREAT GOLF

The South Texas PGA hosts numerous tournaments throughout the year for our section. The tournaments you usually see me playing in are the team events. These events are my favorite because you have a teammate to pick you up in case you have a bad hole along with relieving the pressure of having to finish every hole and post an individual score. Like I've mentioned in previous articles tournament golf is very different from golf with your buddies on Saturday. This tournament, the pro-assistant, allowed me to play with all three of my assistant professionals and my score would be the swing score. If my score is a birdie on a hole and my assistants, make par all three teams count my birdie. Conversely, if my score is bogey and one of my assistants makes par and the other two make bogey, we are able to count par for one team, but bogey is the score for the other two teams.

After dropping my boys off at school and traffic being horrific my car pulled through the gates at Shadow Hawk with no time to hit golf balls and only a few minutes to roll a few putts. We drove to the seventh hole to start our day with a 173-yard hole playing dead into a 20-mph wind. The golf course was soaked from all the rain over the past month and the high winds would make the round more difficult than normal. My first shot of the day was a poorly struck seven iron missing the green, but with a good chip and nice putt made par. As the round continued my shots became crisp and penetrated through the gusty winds with my swing feeling effortless. Growing up in Oklahoma the wind was something that was common pretty much year-round so playing a tournament with high wind felt like an advantage. This was fun to hit knock-down shots and adjust my game to the conditions we were playing under. When the round was over my assistant Colton had holed out for an eagle and made some clutch shots to help us finish one shot short of winning the tournament. My other two assistants played well but were a few shots back from the 66 with team Colton.

It was so much fun to spend the day with my guys who are an integral part of the golf operation and help make Whispering Pines great. Even though we spend long hours together every day we seldom play golf together in the same group. I'm aware of how hard my guys work and try to get them out a few times a season and play together at different courses on Monday's for team building but playing in a tournament with them against teams in our section is even more fun.

After the round it's customary for me to go through my scorecard to see what my I shot if it was a good day. After totaling the round there were four birdies made and had shot 72 in really difficult conditions. The crazy thing about this round was I hadn't hit one golf ball on the range and hadn't played more than three rounds in the past few weeks leading up to this tournament. This got me thinking about why my game came together so well for no apparent reason. There wasn't any new swing tip or adjustment to my game that would warrant a really good tournament round. My conclusion was watching the final round of the PGA Tour event the day before on television. Being golf professional, you would think I'm watching every round of golf on television every week. This is the furthest thing from reality! If it is the Masters or the Colonial, I'm on the couch for sure watching the final round, but outside of those events I'm probably finding out the next day who won.

Bryson DeChambeau won the Shriners PGA Tour event Sunday and was swinging so beautifully that I ended up watching the entire tournament. The way he was calculating and articulating every shot was inspiring to watch. After my round at Shadow Hawk, I realized my shot process and dissection of each shot had subconsciously mimicked Bryson's final round the day before. Watching so many of Bryson's great shots actually changed the way my round probably would have gone in my tournament if my Sunday hadn't been spent watching all his birdies. When Tiger Woods won the Masters in 2000 my experience was coincidentally the same. Watching Tiger's rhythm and execution at Augusta helped me shoot under par the next day at Shady Oaks in a money game with some other pros. The correlation between my two rounds that are eighteen years apart seem simple to understand today. Once again there had been no practice and the last round was three weeks earlier. Watching a professional golfer go through his round in complete control subconsciously helped me imitate what I had seen the day before. I'm not saying every golfer can lay on the couch all afternoon on Sunday and expect to go win a golf tournament on Monday, but you can get better by emulating their pre-shot routine, concentration, and execution.

Next time you watch a PGA Tour event pay attention to what the leader is doing and how they are going through their pre-shot routine. Watch how their concentration level is higher on every shot and tempo and rhythm is sequenced. The best players in the world have tendency that should be copied by the average golfer. You might have one of your best rounds ever if you mimic what you saw the PGA Tour winner do from your couch on Sunday afternoon.

WHAT HOLE IS KILLING YOUR ROUND AND HOW TO GET PAST IT!

We all have the hole on our home course we just can't seem to play well. It might be a very difficult hole or could be a hole that isn't that difficult, but you seem to always make a high score. How do we get past our achilleas heel on the golf course? The first step is to determine where the mistakes are occurring. If you realize your mistakes are strategic you should try looking at different options with your decision process. One example of this is our fifth hole at Whispering Pines which plays as a par five from the one pine tee at 511 yards. Water comes into play if a drive goes more than 260 yards down the left side, but the hole allows for a 300-yard drive to the right side. The challenge with aiming down the right side with driver is you bring the water into play if the drive is pulled and native grass to the right if drive is pushed. The landing area is very small, and the risk is high trying to hit a big drive. The way you play the tee shot is obviously based on how far you hit your driver and how much risk you want to take.

There are a few holes at Whispering Pines that I've managed to birdie more than others. The fifth hole is an example of playing a hole correctly, based on the distance of my tee shots, and reaping the benefits with birdie or par most every round. My driver, when struck well, goes 290 yards under typical conditions. My hybrid goes 245 yards under typical conditions. Every time I play the fifth hole at Whispering Pines it's hybrid off the tee, hybrid second shot, leaving me between 80 and 50 yards for my third shot. Hitting hybrid off the tee takes the water out of play so I can aim down the middle of the fairway and never worry about pulling it left into the water because the water isn't reachable with this club. My second shot is another hybrid, which can't reach the furthest bunker guarding the right side of the green. Playing to my strengths, my wedge game, gives me the best opportunity to score. Hitting all three of these shots mediocre still gives me a good opportunity to make birdie. Conversely hitting a perfect drive and trying to land a hybrid on a green that runs away from you isn't an easy task and doesn't guarantee you making birdie or eagle.

There are many holes on your home course you might play differently if you think about playing them from a statistical and strategic standpoint. Look at your past twenty rounds and find the holes that tend to give you trouble and rethink how you play them. If you change your strategy you just might find the hole that gives you the most trouble becomes one of your favorites!

WHAT'S THE **YARDAGE?**

Every time I'm playing and ask the caddie what's my yardage? I always say, "That's my favorite yardage! ". The caddie starts to look at me funny after a few holes after I've said this phrase more than once from different yardages. My philosophy is whatever yardage I have it's my favorite yardage. This phrase gives me a positive thought before the shot and verbalizing this creates a picture of a successful result. Try this every time your caddie gives you the yardage and I guarantee you will hit better shots!

WHEN VISITING A FAMOUS COURSE

Working at Colonial for ten years and now Whispering Pines for the past fifteen it's common for guests to purchase multiple shirts and hats. Top 100 golf courses tend to sell a lot of merchandise because of their logo and notoriety. Just like buying a rock t-shirt from a great concert to show off that you attended the show the same holds true with club logos from a great course. If you have played Pine Valley and you see another guy wearing a Pine Valley shirt you instantly have a connection. If you see a guy wearing a Van Halen t-shirt it creates a talking point about the band or concert you've seen. Listed below is the rule of thumb when visiting a top 100 golf course.

FOOD & BEVERAGE

Always order the specialty cocktail and the menu item your server recommends as the club's famous go to food. If you are visiting Pine Valley you have to order the snapper soup. If you visit Castle Pines, you have to order the milk shake and when visiting the Olympic Club, you better have at least two of their famous burger dogs.

Golf Shop:

Stay away from the latest trend shirts as trends come and go. The odds of you playing the famous course again might not happen and you don't want a shirt with crazy patterns in your closet for the next ten years. Always purchase a white, navy, or black solid shirt as they never go out of style, along with a sweater as they can be worn for many years.

Caddies:

Always request a veteran caddie for the stories and history lesson about the course. Caddies who've worked at a famous golf course for many years can make the experience memorable and fun regardless of how you played.

I've played a large amount of the top 100 courses in America, but still missing Augusta National from my list. If you have an opportunity to play Augusta and need a fourth, I promise to buy you a white shirt with the Augusta National logo!

WHEN YOU PEEK, YOU PUSH

When you have a putt and peek you usually miss. When the head moves you tend to move the body as well. Most people push putts when they peek. If you find yourself missing putts to the right, try and keep your head still for two seconds before looking. When your head stays still your putting stroke is more consistent.

YOU NEVER KNOW WHEN YOUR GAME MIGHT TURNAROUND

Last week we had we had our North South Match at Whispering Pines. This is an extraordinarily fun event with our members from the Dallas area playing our members from the Houston area. I'm the captain of the north team and play in the event each year. Whispering Pines has a fantastic membership and the camaraderie amongst teams is special, but make no doubt about it, each team really wants to beat the other. The last day of the events format is played as singles matches. We went off as the first tee time and my group had two of my good friends, Dave playing for the North and Cam playing for the south playing alongside my match. Both of the guys take lessons from me and I was cheering for both to play great. I wasn't sure where the match stood at the time, but it looked like the south had won the front nine as we started the back nine. As the match arrived at the fourteenth hole Dave hit an extremely fat wedge sending his ball fifty yards short of the green. The club happened to fly up in the air with an angry stare looking back towards me. With a very sincere statement Dave said, "What am I doing wrong?" Jokingly and trying to lighten the mood said, "I didn't witness the shot, but it looks like we need extra sand for the divot you made." Dave was so upset he was talking about quitting the game as he walked to his ball.

After losing the fourteenth hole, we stood on the fifteenth hole calculating the yardage. The fifteenth is one of the most beautiful par threes you will ever play. The hole was playing 134 yards with a front pin placement. The wind was swirling making club selection very difficult to hit the tiny island green. I was first to play and hit nine iron to eight feet just below the hole. Dave, still steaming from his play on the previous hole, teed up his ball and started his pre-shot routine. He chose nine iron and hit the most beautiful shot you've ever seen. The compression from the club impacting the ball sounded like a PGA Tour player as the ball soared towards the flag. The ball landed a few feet from the hole and spun right in for an ace! We all cheered and gave Dave high fives. It was a remarkable shot and amazing to witness in person.

The next three holes Dave managed to play incredible golf and won the back nine shooting one under par over the last four holes. After the fourteenth hole it looked like there was no way he could win the back nine. After the hole in one Dave's attitude completely changed and he played a totally different game on the final holes. At one moment he was ready to quit the game and five minutes later we are celebrating the ultimate shot. One shot can change an entire round sometimes for good like Dave's hole in one or sometimes bad like his poor shot on the fourteenth hole. I've never made a hole in one and have played golf all my life, but I've had rounds where something good happened and changed the rest of my round. You never know when something good is going to happen on the golf course, so regardless of how bad your round might be stay positive and your next shot might be like Dave's.

MY SCOTTISH CADDY

A few weeks ago, I traveled across the pond to the British Open with one of my golf buddies. If you've never been to this tournament you need to put it on your bucket list. The game is played completely different than it's played in the United States. The PGA Tour courses reward high towering shots into receptive greens where the links courses require the player to hit shots short and allow them to run to the pin. Most people watching on television would think the golf course looks like a run-down municipal track in your home city, but it's far from that. This is where golf was invented, and the skills needed to plot your way around these links takes shot making to another level.

During the week you go to the pro shop and stock up on shirts and caps to bring back as mementos of your major championship week. The fish and chips are the best you will ever taste. I'm not sure what they do different, but in four days I ate them five times. The Scottish people are fun, and their knowledge of the game is admirable. There is something about Scotland that will have me returning for many future visits.

You can't go to Scotland and not bring your clubs so tee times were made at Kingsbarns and the Jubilee course at St. Andrews. Kingsbarns is the Pebble Beach of Europe and had many breathtaking views. St. Andrews breathes history and the clubhouse at the Royal Ancient stands as the focal point of this charming town.

The day we played the Jubilee at St. Andrews we were introduced to our caddy named John. He had an extreme Scottish accent and numerous times I had to ask him what he had just said. John laughed at my Texas accent and said if you ever bumped into the caddies at the pub after a few pints you really wouldn't understand what he was saying. He was very knowledgeable and fun to be with for the round. He told me a story on the 13th hole that really struck a chord with me and made me want to write about.

John caddies for a man who is blind and described how he lines him up towards his target and describes the shot needed. This fascinated me and led to me asking him numerous golf questions from an instructor's perspective. The thing that stood out the most was John talking about his job of describing the hole to his player as he adjusted his alignment and put the club head behind the ball. He mentioned for the first six months of working for this golfer he would describe in great detail of the trouble that was in front of him. John would describe the entire hole, but he focused on the trouble like the bunkers or out of bounds. Even though the golfer was lined up in the direction he was supposed to hit his shot he would tend to hit the shot where John had described the trouble. One day John changed his approach and told his blind golfer there wasn't any trouble to worry about and only described where he wanted him to hit the shot. Instead of telling the golfer where he didn't want to hit his shot, he told him where he wanted to hit his shot. Remember the blind golfer could only go by what his caddy was describing.

The mind is an amazing thing and the thoughts you have standing over the golf ball will produce what you think. There is no such thing as muscle memory, only your brain can remember, but you can choose the thoughts you think. Just like John telling the blind golfer about all the bad things that could happen to his shot it created an image where he saw bunkers and out of bounds. When John told him only the places where he wanted to hit his shot the blind golfers score improved dramatically.

You can't make the out of bounds and bunkers physically go away, but you can choose to think about the good things when you set up for your next shot. I'm going to think about fairways and greens after hanging out in Scotland for eighteen holes with John.

NEVER AIM WHERE A STRAIGHT BALL COULD GET YOU IN TROUBLE

Most golfers curve the ball one way or the other and the straight ball is much like a hole in one, rarely seen. Very few players in the history of the game have hit a straight ball as their primary shot. Nicklaus predominantly hit a fade, Arnold Palmer mainly played a draw and 99% of every golfer does the same. Hogan once said a straight ball at Colonial will get you in more trouble than any course in the country. The reason Mr. Hogan said this is because Colonial has very few straight holes. Almost every hole on the course outside of par threes have sharp doglegs at the corners of each fairway. If you are hitting the ball straight at Colonial, you typically are driving the ball through the fairways solidifying Mr. Hogan's assessment of the course.

When you play a hole, you should always pick a line that allows wiggle room for your shot to curve right or left. When you pick a line that doesn't allow for a straight shot you should change the direction you would like your shot to start. The ninth hole at Whispering Pines is a great example of choosing the correct line for the tee shot. The hole is a slight dogleg to the right with two bunkers guarding the left side of the fairway and one bunker guarding the right. People who aim at the bunkers on the left and their shot doesn't fade end up in the deep bunkers. Conversely if you choose to try and fly the bunker on the right to cut off yardage and your ball doesn't draw you end up in this deep bunker. Never aim directly at trouble hoping your ball will curve away. Rather always pick a line that a straight ball would be perfect and if the ball fades or draws you would still be alright for your next shot.

NEW AND IMPROVED

How many times can you make something new and improved? You watch any commercial and something is labeled new and improved. Is my toothpaste really better this year than it was two years ago? How about the cleaning detergent? We've been told that everything is better than it was before in hopes of us purchasing the product being marketed.

Golf instructors use these same marketing techniques as well. Is there really a new and improved method that is radically going to change your game? There is no cookie cutter solution to a golf swing, but everyone on the PGA Tour chases the next hot idea. My main man, Bryson DeChambeau now looks like the hulk and is slashing away at the ball with massive distance gains. I'm not sure everyone on tour will go to the extremes that Bryson goes, but many will if he has success. If my lessons started involving me wearing flip flops and having my assistant turn your hips while holding them from behind, would that make you better? The hot player usually means their teacher is hot and in demand. This is how the instructor charges $1000.00 per hour because he showed an extremely talented golfer how to do something he could already perform. Do you remember stack & tilt, one-plane, X factor and all the other teaching techniques that have come along in the past few decades? How many of these techniques do you currently hear about today? The golf swing is simple, yet complex. When you play well everything seems so easy and then there are days where nothing works. I've heard you never own your golf swing, but you can rent it. Byron Nelson said *"find a swing that works for you and spend the rest of your life trying to repeat it."*

The reason for writing this story isn't to knock any golf instructor, but more for the student to understand everything they read or hear isn't necessarily the correct solution for their game. Anytime a first-time student leaves my teaching facility they are asked a couple of questions. Did you enjoy the lesson? Did you learn something? If the answer is yes on both then I've done my job with the student. As an instructor you should be able to help the student play better golf in one lesson. The chiropractic approach is asking the student to come back six more times and your flaw will be gone. If you have a golf instructor tell you this you should move on down the range and ask for another instructor. We need to be accountable to the student. If you go see the doctor it's his job to figure out and diagnose the problem. If the doctor tells me to take the same medication on three different visits and I'm not better, it would be crazy to go back for a fourth visit. The reason Butch Harmon is the best instructor in the world is because he doesn't have any specific swing he teaches. He builds the players confidence and finds the flaw causing the most issue. Dustin Johnson's golf swing doesn't look like

Brooks Koepka's swing nor does Greg Norman's swing look like Tiger's.

Work with your instructor to find the swing you can consistently repeat and stay away from every new fad that comes along in the golf world!

PARENTING ATHLETES

I'm not saying my parenting skills are perfect and I'm still a work in progress with my two teenagers as this is being written, but my oldest son has started his professional career, which has given me some time to reflect. Dylan has always been a good athlete with every sport he tried. He chose golf as his career path and when he asked my opinion of his decision it made me extremely happy as his father. The first thing he was told by dad when he made this decision was, *I will get you to the front of the line in the golf business and you have to do the rest.* He has seen the perks and blessings of being a Golf Professional at one of the top clubs in the country, but he didn't see the seventy-hour work weeks it takes to get to the top. He is now living the seventy-hour work weeks at Valhalla in Kentucky and recently landed a winter job at Seminole in Florida.

I've coached hundreds of kids during my career and have worked with many overbearing parents, who live their dreams through their children. One rule I have when working with a junior golfer whose parent wants to watch the lesson, is *we are all going to be a team.* It's made clear during the first lesson that I'm the coach and the parent is the parent, and we will all work in the best interest of the student. I've mentioned many times to the parent if you see something your child is doing incorrectly tell them *remember what your coach said about the flaw.* When the parent starts telling their child what they are doing wrong it seldom goes well for either of them. We have all seen the young golfer under the critical eye of their parent or the lunatic baseball dad who yells at the umpire during a little league game. If you want your child to succeed let them enjoy the process rather than forcing them to love a sport. The great ones don't have to be pushed.

Dylan went to a private school and all the parents would drive to the basketball games, much like you saw in the movie Hoosiers. The kids rode the bus to the game but could ride home with their parents after the game. Some of my fondest memories were those late-night drives back to Huntsville after a game. Dylan was a really good three-point shooter and averaged over thirty points for much of his last two years playing basketball. When he would get in the car after a game, we would always discuss the highlights and I would listen to his thoughts. I've always made it a point to compliment him about all the things he did well and tell him how proud he made me. Never did I start out the conversation by telling him everything he did wrong. Most parents of athletes go straight to this strategy when they talk to their child after a sporting event. It never took more than five minutes for Dylan to ask me what he could have done better in the game. This gave me the opportunity to tell him what he could improve on without being the father who critiques their child on their every move. Starting with compliments and waiting for your child to ask you your thoughts is a wonderful way to be a parent to your child athlete. Their success doesn't rely on a competitive score because whatever game they play will eventually come to an end, but you will always be there parent long after the last pitch, free throw or putt is holed.

PEOPLE RARELY REMEMBER YOUR SHOTS

The past few months I've played a lot of golf with my members. We've had a home and home match against the Preserve Golf Club in California, Robertson Cup at Whispering Pines, and our North South matches last week. Each of these events allowed me to play 54 holes with different members and allowed me to get my game in pretty good shape. It dawned on me that I have zero recollection of any score or outcome of any match. We often think our playing partners are analyzing each shot we hit and judging our game. As the golf professional I feel pressure to play well with every member, but my main focus is helping my members with their games and giving them an enjoyable experience. I've seen members get so uptight and play bad rounds because they are worried about what their playing partners might think of their swing or score. The truth is nobody really cares! We are all focused on our own game and have our own insecurities about our swing or score. If you asked the guys you played with last weekend what you shot, they probably couldn't tell you. If you were asked what they shot you probably couldn't tell them either. The next time you tee it up don't worry about what people think, rather focus on enjoying the company you're with and realize next week they have no idea what you shot.

PGA TOUR PLAYERS

When the PGA Tour would come to Fort Worth it was always enlightening to see some PGA Tour player's hit shots like the average guy. If you like watching the final round of a PGA Tour event or Major Championships, you only see three or four groups on the television coverage. The final few groups on Sunday are hitting fantastic shots, making every putt, and make the game look simple. The reality is these guys are playing some of the best golf of their year. They don't always play great and they all have struggles like the rest of us playing this game. The next time you have an opportunity to attend a PGA Tour event, go out on a Thursday and you will see some shots that might surprise you. Don't get me wrong PGA Tour players could beat 99% of us on their worst day, but they still hit some bad shots and miss some short putts.

The next time you hit an embarrassing shot and feel like you are the only person this has ever happened to understand that some PGA Tour players have hit that same shot!

PLAY THE FORWARD TEES TO GAIN CONFIDENCE

Last week one our members asked me to play nine holes with him and his guests. This particular member likes to play our three pine markers, which are considered our senior tees at Whispering Pines. As the Golf Professional it's customary to play the tees the member plays when asked to accompany them for a round. Playing from such a short yardage it was evident my driver wouldn't be used very much, if any during the nine holes. On the first hole, which is a dogleg left par four, I teed off with a seven-iron leaving me 110 yards to the pin. Taking a gap wedge, my shot came off crisp landing one foot from the hole. The second hole is a par five where I hit hybrid off the tee leaving me 204 yards from the pin. With a solid four iron my ball came to rest fifteen feet from the cup for an eagle attempt. I'm not going to go through the rest of the round but making four birdies and missing two birdie putts from four feet definitely gave me confidence.

Playing from the forward tees makes you play differently than you would playing the regular tees at your home course. Even though driver wasn't the proper play on the majority of the holes, it allowed me to hit shorter clubs to specific areas of the fairway and have shorter shots into the green. Hitting a nine iron into a green where you usually would hit six iron really allowed me to go pin seeking. The golf course was much shorter, but you still had to hit quality shots to score well.

If you are struggling with your confidence or preparing for an upcoming tournament go out and play nine holes from the forward tees. Seeing birdie putts drop and shooting a lower score than usual can really boost your confidence. When you go back to your regular tees you will have some positive mojo and hopefully a lower score!

PLAYING SCARED

Have you ever been scared to hit a certain shot on the course? We've all had some shot that made us cringe when we approached the ball. Some of you it's a bunker shot to a tight pin with little green to work with. Some of you it's the tee shot with trouble on the right and a left to right wind. Even the simple chip shot sometimes can debilitate the PGA Tour player.

Tiger Woods had the chip yips, Ernie Els had the yips on the green, and Ian Baker Finch completely lost his ability to compete after a demoralizing day with Arnold Palmer in the British Open where he shot 91.

The only players who conquer their fear are those who continue to work on their flaw and continue to try the shot they fear in competition. The moment you give in to fear you usually will resort to trying to avoid embarrassment. This is something you can't allow in your game! If you have chipping issues you can't pull out a seven iron or hybrid to chip when the only way to get the shot close is to use a sand wedge. I've seen a player who could hit fifteen greens in regulation but had absolutely no chance of getting up and down for a par on the three greens he missed. Every time he would pull out a hybrid and try to run the ball up a slope and pray it stopped within ten feet so he might be able to make the putt. This guy was a fantastic player but wouldn't pull a wedge out for any shot around the green out of fear.

Players who play scared usually have a flaw in their technique or swing and then it becomes mental over time. Once the brain starts thinking of all the bad things that can happen instead of what good things can happen you have started playing scared.

Get with your instructor and ask him to help you with the shots you fear the most. Get sound fundamentals along with practice drills to start the process of overcoming your fear. Once you can hit the shots in a practice setting take it to the course and see if you can hit those shots. Eliminating your fear is a process and doesn't' happen overnight. Start the process today and don't play scared anymore!

PRESIDENT BUSH

When President George W. Bush arrived on property at Whispering Pines it was a day I'll never forget. In the golf industry you meet many celebrities, and it is always fun to have them on property. Of all the famous people who've come through the clubs where I've worked none were more memorable than #43 coming to the pines. Our owner let us know a few weeks before about a special guest coming on property on a Tuesday in June when the club was closed.

Only a few of the staff were allowed at the club that day and the secret service was all over the property. The only negative to the entire day was it was absolutely the hottest day I've ever witnessed in Trinity. The humidity was so high the windows of the professional shop were steamed over.

The Presidential motorcade as it rolled through our gates was very impressive. One by one black Chevy Suburban's pulled into the parking lot with secret service detail all exiting the vehicles as President Bush stepped out and walked into the professional shop. In a Texas drawl President Bush said, "Let's get the pictures taken and autographs signed and go play some golf." The President went to the range with the sun permeating on all of us he said, "It's going to be a heater today boys" and began to hit range balls. Standing there watching the most powerful man in world hit golf shots as he asked my critique of his ball flight was beyond amazing. Never in my wildest dreams did I think hanging out with President Bush would be in my list of cool things to do before you die.

As the day continued to get hotter, our owner Mr. Robertson asked me to bring out some iced mango towels to help the group cool off. On the eighth hole, Mr. Robertson asked me to bring the group some of our new moisture wicking shirts from the professional shop. Another moment you never forget is bringing four shirts to the ninth green having the entire group take off their sweat drenched shirts and replace them with dry Whispering Pines shirts. Whispering Pines isn't Preston Trail where it is acceptable to play golf without a shirt, but President Bush is a member of Preston Trail so maybe that's why he prompted the shirt change on the green rather than the clubhouse. Either way it was another story to include on this special day.

When we reached the 15th hole a jet ski came by going up Caney Creek, which is adjacent to the hole. As the jet ski zoomed past the tee box and headed up the creek, I looked at our distinguished guest and said, "Mr. President that guy got on his jet ski today in Trinity, Texas and he's going up the river thinking to himself there's no way that was President Bush." He smiled and hit his shot in the center of the island green. As we made our way around to the green, we saw the jet ski heading back to Lake Livingston. When we approached the green the secret service all stood on the bank observing in case the person came back. This was humorous to me because this was a country boy who had no idea what he had just witnessed while enjoying his day on the lake. As the secret service stood watching for a jet ski and we stood watching President Bush stroke his putt for a possible birdie the line of my golf career was delivered. President Bush barely missed the putt and picked up his ball from a few inches away and said, "Boys we need to hurry up and get off this green because my secret service thinks that's Al-Qaeda on a jet ski trying to kill me!" He then followed that up by saying "If it was Al-Qaeda we would have a cruiser come down the creek and blow his ass out of the water." Everyone started laughing as we made our way to the sixteenth hole.

Of all my days in the golf business there is no other day that stands out more than this day hanging with #43 at the pines. He was thoughtful, asked questions about my family and made sure everyone received some quality time with him. Politics aside there was no doubt this President loved his country and would do anything to protect the United States. If you read the book "Decision Points" it's undeniable this man did the best he could under extreme circumstances during his presidency. He admits his mistakes in the book and without question went to bed every night with the enormous weight of protecting this country on his mind. When people ask me, who was the most famous person I've met in the golf industry it's always an easy answer and it's one letter "W."

RUBBERNECKING

We've all been there stuck in traffic and wondering what has happened in front of us to cause the backup. When we finally reach the fender bender a few miles later we all stop look at the accident. This is called rubbernecking and for the life of me I'm not sure why we all do this. This act slows down traffic and sometimes we witness things we wish we wouldn't have.

In golf you sometimes have one of your fellow competitors have a wreck on the course that causes a backup to the round. It is fine to help someone look for their golf ball when they are struggling but rubbernecking on the golf course will not do your game any good. When we watch someone struggle it sometimes rubs off on our own game. You see this all the time on the PGA Tour where a star group like Rory, Tiger and Mickelson are playing together and they all have bad days. Conversely you see another star pairing like Kutcher, Thomas and Fowler all get off to great starts and feed off each other having great rounds.

Watching your fellow competitor hit great shots is fine and can even inspire your game but watching them miss short putts or struggle with chipping can affect your own game. Every day on a highway in Texas there are hundreds of cars rubbernecking to see an accident. Every day God gives us a beautiful sunset to admire as well. Too often we gawk at the accident and miss the sunsets.

Stop the rubbernecking on the highway and you will get to your destination sooner. Stop watching your fellow competitors wreck and you will play better.

SELLING MY HOUSE

Selling a home is stressful to say the least and keeping the house in great shape through this process is even more stressful with two teenage boys visiting every other weekend. Both my kids decided they want to live with dad and in order for this to work my house would have to go on the market so I could move to their school district. This has been my prayer for the last six years and the house went on the market as soon as the boys asked to live with me.

When you are selling your house you always have to have everything looking perfect in your home. You don't leave dirty dishes out. You vacuum and dust on a regular basis and never let your kids leave the house without making their bed. This is what we all should do, but let's face it we don't always keep everything in our home in perfect condition. The number of times my realtor sent a text for a showing in the next two hours happened on a regular basis. My rule to my kids was to keep the house in show condition always and we would never have to scramble to make it look good when the realtor wanted to show it.

What if we took the same approach to our golf game as we would do in keeping our house in showroom shape? How many times have you been invited to play with a group on Saturday morning, after someone dropped out, and felt your game wasn't ready? How many times has someone invited you on a golf trip at the last minute and you wished you had been practicing? Most of us go into panic mode when this happens and usually don't play our best golf. Conversely, I've worked with clients who have a big golf trip to Pebble Beach or Scotland and start preparing months in advance. The golfer who prepares ahead of time usually hits a lot of good shots and enjoys the trip much more when they put in the practice time. Everyone has different levels of enjoyment in their golf game. Some of my students work very hard and are not satisfied if they don't play well and some of my students just want to keep from embarrassing themselves and enjoy the camaraderie. Whatever your reasons for playing the game, it's always more fun to hit good shots.

My challenge to each player is to always keep your game in decent shape and it won't take much work to get it in good shape. Much like my house has been in decent shape for the past year and only took minimal time to make it look great if the realtor called. Don't let your house get too messy and don't let your game get to the point where your golf realtor doesn't want to show your swing.

The house sold this week and construction will start on my new home in a few weeks. A new journey begins in a new town, with a new home, and most importantly with my two boys!

SHOULD YOU TAKE A LESSON IF YOU ARE PLAYING GREAT?

This question seems simple and the obvious answer would be why would you need a lesson if you are playing well? When you are playing your best golf, this is a perfect opportunity to have your instructor document your numbers on trackman and get video of your swing. I've done this with numerous students over the years after they have won an event. Robert Thompson is the only player to ever win PGA Q School and Senior PGA Q School. If you want to win a bet throw that question out to a group of golfers in the nineteenth hole! Robert has allowed me to be his eyes from time to time for touch ups for his golf game and like most great players when they get off track it's usually the same technical flaw. Robert had just won the Senior Club Professional Championship and was playing some incredible golf. The next time he was at the club I asked him to come into the teaching facility and allow me to film a few swings and save them for future reference. He obliged but didn't want to see his swing on video. A few years later Robert was preparing for another big tournament and asked me to look at his swing. He was struggling and the probability of him playing a great tournament didn't look promising. Noticing the issue, I told him to hit a few shots on film and then compared them to my saved footage from the previous year when he was playing incredible golf. Comparing the two swings side by side on my computer screen he could see his posture had changed and swing plane was a few degrees off. Making the slight adjustment he started hitting the ball fantastic again because he was able to see it for himself on video. Saving the great swings allowed us to have a reference point to always go back to when he struggles with his game. I've done this with numerous students over my golf career and it has always allowed for a reference point to go back to for corrections. PGA Tour players do this all the time with their coaches and even replay tournaments they've won to see if they can pick up anything, they were doing different then versus now.

I'm a huge Jordan Spieth fan and like all of us in Texas we are hoping for a resurgence in his game. It would be advantageous for Jordan to watch every tournament round where he won. When you have four days of documentation of winning The Masters rewind the DVR and watch every putt drop and every drive striped down the fairway. Having documentation to go back to not only helps with swing issues it can help you regain your confidence and form when you were playing your best.

The next time you are playing great golf and the swing feels solid book a lesson with your instructor and have him document everything you are doing well in your game!

SIMULATE SITUATIONS BEFORE THEY HAPPEN

You hear of football coaches, who are going into a loud hostile environment, piping in extremely loud music during their practice leading up to the game. Football coaches also have their defense simulate their opponent schemes during practice leading up to the big game. Why do the coaches do this? It's obvious they want their team to have been in the situations they are going to be in before they are actually in them. This is what I refer to as the Deja Vu moment when coaching golfers. Feeling like you've already been in the situation helps you perform better when you actually are in the situation.

At the end of a lesson, it's common that my student is told for their last shot of the session they have to hit a shot on the green to win their upcoming tournament. This is the same target the student has been hitting to for the majority of the lesson. It's amazing how many times the shot is so far from hitting the target! The entire lesson they've hit shot after shot to a target, but simulated pressure changes rhythm and mechanics. If you can't hit the shot on the driving range, you're probably not going to hit the shot on the course when it counts. After the shot has missed the target, I ask the student a few questions. Did you feel pressure on that shot? Did the target move? Did you change clubs? Did a huge gust of wind come up? The student always looks at me and answers each question with a puzzled look. The target didn't move, the wind didn't change, they didn't hit a different club, but they all answer *yes* about feeling pressure.

It's so common to see golfers on the range hitting random shots without aiming at a specific target. I've asked thousands of students over the years, while walking down the line of the driving range, what are you aiming at on this shot? The popular answer *"I'm just warming up and not aiming at anything."* My question to them is *"Are you going to aim at anything on the golf course when you go to the first tee?"* If you aim at nothing you will hit it every time!

When you practice you should always simulate what you will face on the course that day or in an upcoming event. Every shot should be to a specific target with the club that produces the correct yardage.

When you plan a trip to Pebble Beach you know the greens are the smallest on tour so you shouldn't practice sixty-foot putts the week before your trip. Conversely, if you are playing Champions Golf Club in Houston you should spend plenty of time working on long putts due to the size of their greens.

Plan your practice sessions around the type of course and conditions you will be playing. If you're favorite football team is playing the Seahawks in Seattle you better hope your coach is piping in some loud music during practice. . Every practice session should be conducted for the soul purpose of how you want to play your next round of golf. If you are headed to the range this afternoon work on the shots, you will most likely encounter during your next round and you will probably play well!

STOP SWEEPING THE DIRT UNDER THE RUG

It's easy to sweep dirt under the rug, but eventually you are going to have a pile of dirt to clean up. We all do this in our golf games at times. You know you should call your pro and ask them to look at your swing. Let's put it off until next week is the normal reaction most golfer have. We come to realize the more we put the lesson off the more dirt tends to pile up in our swing. Over the years I've given many lessons where the student said they were going to come see me but kept putting it off. When these students finally come in the teaching facility there is usually much more work needing to be done on their swing because they have put it off too long. Conversely the student who realizes they have gotten into some bad habits and books a lesson as soon as their schedule allows tends to not go into slumps.

Sweep the floors once a month and you might have a lot of dirt in your dustpan. Sweep every week and you will have much less dirt in your dustpan. If your golf swing gets off track don't wait for the dirt to pile up to go, see your golf professional!

SWISS ARMY KNIFE

Most adult men over the age of 40 probably had a Swiss army knife when they were growing up. Phillips screwdriver, bottle opener, wood saw, and scissors were common tools you would find on one of these knives. Pretty much anything that might happen on a camping trip your trusty Swiss army knife should be able to handle the situation.

The fourteen clubs in your golf bag are your tools for a round of golf. They all serve a purpose as well and each has a specific shot they produce. You might not use your lob wedge for an entire round but need it for a plugged bunker shot the next time you play. You might not use the scissors on your Swiss army for several camping trips and then need it when you need to cut something. All fourteen clubs will be used at some point over the course of a golf season so it's important to keep them sharp. If we only keep certain clubs sharp, then we can't have the confidence needed when we encounter a shot we haven't practiced.

Make sure and work with each club in your bag to keep them sharp just like you would make sure your Swiss army knife tools were sharp if you were going on a two-week camping trip. You never know what situation you might encounter, but keeping your tools sharp gives you a better chance for success at the campground and the golf course.

TAKE A BROOKS KOEPKA ATTITUDE TO THE COURSE

Brooks Koepka, undoubtedly, is one of the best golfers in the world as this story is being written. One of the things that Brooks uses as motivation is the press and their unwillingness to give him the love he deserves after two incredible seasons on the PGA Tour. Adding injury to insult he was recently slighted again amongst his peers and came in second to Rory McIlroy for player of the year. This guy has had a hall of fame career in a two-year span and continues to get better, but still seems to lack the respect he deserves. Some players would get distraught about this, but Brooks uses these situations as opportunities to shove it back in his naysayer's face.

The Robertson Cup is an event we host at Whispering Pines every year and invite top 100 clubs from all over the country to participate. The format is a pro-am with one PGA Professional bringing three of his members for three days of competition and fun. Because it would be easy to find out the golf professional's name from the highly prestigious club the name of the course will not be mentioned. One of my good friends, who's a member of our club along with the other club, told me his pro and I would get along great, because we were a lot alike. He then mentioned after that comment that his pro wasn't a great player. He wasn't saying this in a malicious way nor did I think he was saying this in a negative way towards my game, but this is the way I took the comment. This gave me motivation during the next few weeks leading up to the tournament. My entire goal and all my practice were geared towards playing a great round with one of my good friends and his golf professional.

Being the host professional for a huge event, along with playing in the event is much like running your own wedding. You are coordinating the course set-up, working with your chef on all the meals, having each cottage have the gifts presented exactly to specifications, giving speeches and then try and make birdies for team Whispering Pines. Over the years I've gotten much better at managing my game while running one of our premiere events, but it's always a challenge to peak your golf game when your primary goal is making sure every team and golf professional has a great time.

The day finally came, and nobody knew anything about the comment made the previous month. My motivation was to play the best golf possible and beat the other professional individually and my team shoots the lower score for the day. My assistant announced our names on the first hole, and I striped a hybrid splitting the center of the fairway. I'm not sure of my score that day, but the round was exactly how I dreamed it up. We played exceptional, shooting the lower score in our foursome and my individual score was lower than the opposing professional. Nobody in the group knew anything about the comment from weeks earlier and until this story it had never been mentioned to anyone.

Motivation is a great tool to get your mind ready to go to battle on the course. You see this in sports all the time when another team or player mocks or makes predictions about a game. You sometimes see a David step up and take down the Goliath when the opponent is overconfident. Brooks Koepka has used this to become one of the best players in the game and on that Monday, morning match my attitude was just like Brooks.

Next time you have a big tournament or match get yourself in the mind-set of being an underdog and play with a chip on your shoulder just like Brooks does on the PGA Tour.

THAT'S A GOODWIN

Bart Goodwin consistently wins our club championship at Whispering Pines Golf Club. To date he has won this event seven times and always the favorite when our club plays this event. Bart has traveled with me all-over the country playing in home and home matches with other clubs. Every single match it is a given Bart will be playing the other team's best player and he usually wins. We have even named a good shot after him called a Goodwin rather than a good one!

His swing is rhythmic and looks wonderful, but that's not the reason is so good. His short game is good even if he constantly talks about his putting problems. He is long, but not extraordinarily long. So, what makes Bart such a good player? His self-belief in his game and experience is why he has won the most club championships at our club. Bart is great in business just as all of our members are, but most of you reading this have more self-belief in your ability to run your business than you might have over a four-foot putt to win a bet. Confidence breeds success and the more confidence you have the better you become at whatever it is you are trying to attain.

What if you put the time in to work on your game with the goal of becoming a great golfer? How would you practice? How many times would you play a round of golf? How many tournaments would you sign up to play?

Everyone is different, but Bart plays in tournaments throughout the year at our club along with amateur events around the country. When he arrives at Whispering Pines, he always spends time hitting balls before and after the round. This is what makes him different than the average golfer trying to win his club championship. When you put in the time and work on the correct things you will eventually achieve results.

The next time you are at Whispering Pines and you hit a good shot it's really a GOODWIN!

THE BIG FIGHT

Lately my television consumption has increased more than any other time in my life. With the corona virus changing the way we live most of us have probably watched more television or read more books in the past month than we would in an entire year. Unfortunately, some of the basketball or football games that I hadn't seen or knew the outcome before tuning in had already been given to me by Dish Network at the bottom of the screen. Why would the satellite companies put the final score of a game at the bottom of the screen before you watch the game? One of the sports they hadn't given out the ending has been boxing and UFC fights. This has provided me plenty of entertainment the past few weeks because the unknown was left for my imagination. Does George Foreman beat Evander Holyfield? Does Conner McGregor win the fight or was this one of the fights he lost? As long as my youngest son doesn't walk in and tell me who wins the UFC fight before it's over the entertainment value is just like watching live.

One of the things I've noticed with all these fights are how conditioned the fighters are when the bell rings. I've pitched a forty-nine-year shutout without ever being in a fight and plan to keep it that way unless an Eagles fan throws beer on me at a Cowboy game. These fighters train for months preparing for their opponent. They study all their strengths and weakness to gain any advantage they can on their opponent. Much like Professional Golfers have a swing coach, short-game coach, mental coach, and dietician in their corner; fighters have trainers and coaches with specific skill sets to help them perform their best when they get in the ring.

Fighters spar with other fighters for months to prepare themselves for the real fight. The coaches will find sparring partners who can simulate the person they are going to eventually fight, and they will usually even be the same build and height. The more realistic the sparring partner is to the real opponent the more seamless the real fight will be on fight night. Can you imagine what would happen if the fighter never sparred before the big fight, but only conditioned and practiced his technique? It probably wouldn't bode well for anyone who took this approach before getting into the ring.

It's interesting how golfers prepare for their club championship or member-guest tournaments. My experience has been most people only want to work on their swing. This is definitely a valid point but swinging well doesn't guarantee shooting low scores or winning. The reason so many players choose to play the Houston Open is mainly due to the date being a week before the Masters and the golf course conditioning is as close to Augusta National as any course on the PGA Tour. This was a genius move on the people who run the Houston Open, because it guaranteed they would get some players that might never play in their event if it weren't for these two factors. The Houston Open essentially created a sparring partner for the PGA Tour players in preparation for The Masters.

So how do you simulate your sparring partner for your club championship or member-guest this year? Whispering Pines held the Texas State Amateur a few years ago and the host club gets three exemptions. The only fair way to decide who would get an exemption was giving the top three finishers in our club championship the spots. We have a lot of good players at Whispering Pines and all of them know the course very well, but the Texas State Amateur would play from the back tees. Whispering Pines is brutally difficult from the back tees and very few members venture all the back to test themselves. The slope rating is 152 with a 77.3 index from the Spirit tees. This means that a scratch player playing very well would shoot around 77 on his best day. I've been the golf professional for sixteen years and the lowest I've ever posted all the way back was a score of 76. All this to say, Whispering Pines is extremely difficult!

The only time we've ever played our club championship from the back tees was the year we hosted the TXAM. Making the decision to brutally test our best players was an easy choice, because playing the back tees would simulate the way the golf course would be played in the amateur. All the members who signed up were made aware of the tees being used for the qualifying process. Many of my students started working with me a month out of the event to prepare. Everyone wants to play in their state amateur and for many of them it would be their best opportunity due to the size of the field and home course knowledge. Every student who took lessons leading up to the tournament had a similar schedule with me. First lesson was getting swing where it needed to be playing from 7443 yards. Second lesson was spent working on longer irons and hybrids coming into the greens for the second shot. Short game was mixed in with all of this, but the final few lessons were spent on the golf course playing the actual tees where the tournament would be played. Some of my students couldn't carry the ball 270 yards so we had to come up with new strategies to be able to compete. Most of my students usually hit mid to short irons into the majority of our par fours from our member tees. This wouldn't be the case in the qualifier, so we hit numerous shots from longer distances to prepare. None of the par five holes would be reachable so working on laying up to correct yardages for their best opportunities with a wedge became imperative.

My approach was to make Whispering Pines from the back tees their sparring partner so they would be prepared. All three of the guys who qualified for the state amateur hit the ball 280 yards off the tee and all of them had to hit hybrids and long irons to the majority of the greens. The final spot was achieved with a three wood for his second shot into the 499-yard 18th hole and then had to sink a long birdie. All three of these guys played numerous practices rounds from the back tees to prepare weeks before the tournament bell rang. They are all good players, but their sparring preparation is what helped them knockout their opponents.

Whispering Pines played like sparring Mike Tyson that week, but it's very unlikely the three guys who qualified would have played as well if they had sparred against Urkel!

CPSIA information can be obtained
at www.ICGtesting.com
Printed in the USA
BVHW040239210522
637574BV00002B/10